KINK IS

An Anthology of Surprisingly Relatable
True Stories About Sex, Power, and Joy

KINK IS

Curated and edited by:
Race Bannon, Patrick Davis,
Jörg Fockele, Silke Niggemeier,
Adam Ouderkirk, Beatrice Stonebanks

UNBOUND EDITION PRESS

Atlanta

Copyright © 2024 by Divine Deviance, LLC
All Rights Reserved

No part of this book may be reproduced, distributed, or transmitted in any form or by any means, including photocopying, recording, or other electronic or mechanical methods, without the prior written permission of the publisher, except in the case of brief quotations embodied in critical reviews and certain other noncommercial uses permitted by copyright law.

FIRST EDITION

Printed in the United States of America

LIBRARY OF CONGRESS RECORD

Name: Bannon, Race, 1954 — editor.
Davis, Patrick, 1966 — editor.
Fockele, Jörg, 1964 — editor.
Niggemeier, Silke, 1975 — editor.
Ouderkirk, Adam, 1961 — editor.
Stonebanks, Beatrice, 1961 — editor.
Title: Kink Is
Edition: First edition.
Published: Atlanta : Unbound Edition Press, 2024.

LCCN: 2024937298
LCCN Permalink: https://lccn.loc.gov/2024937298
ISBN: 979-8-9892333-7-3 (fine softcover)

Designed by Eleanor Safe and Joseph Floresca
Printed by Bookmobile, Minneapolis, MN
Distributed by Itasca Books

123456789

Unbound Edition Press
1270 Caroline Street, Suite D120
Box 448
Atlanta, GA 30307

The Unbound Edition Press logo and name are registered trademarks of Unbound Edition LLC.

Unbound Edition Press champions honest, original voices. Committed to the power of writers who explore and illuminate the contemporary human condition, we publish collections of poetry, short fiction, and essays. Our publisher and editorial team aim to identify, develop, and defend authors who create thoughtfully challenging work which may not find a home with mainstream publishers. We are guided by a mission to respect and elevate emerging, under-appreciated, and marginalized authors, with a strong commitment to advancing LGBTQ+ and BIPOC voices. We are honored to make meaningful contributions to the literary arts by publishing their work.

For information on bulk purchases, academic course adoptions, or community reading group copies, please contact Unbound Edition Press at inquiry@unboundedition.com or use the "Contact" form on our website. Examination copies are available for professors considering this book for course adoption.

To discuss potential excerpt or citation use, translation rights, or international rights, please contact us by using the same methods noted above.

unboundedition.com

ABOUT THE TYPE AND PAPER

Designed by Malou Verlomme of the Monotype Studio, Macklin is an elegant, high-contrast typeface. It has been designed purposely for more emotional appeal.

The concept for Macklin began with research on historical material from Britain and Europe dating to the beginning of the 19th century, specifically the work of Vincent Figgins. Verlomme pays respect to Figgins's work with Macklin, but pushes the family to a more contemporary place.

This book is printed on natural Rolland Enviro Book stock. The paper is 100 percent post-consumer sustainable fiber content and is FSC-certified.

Kink Is was designed by Eleanor Safe and Joseph Floresca.

To help fund a series of short documentary films based on *Kink Is*, please consider making a donation to our non-profit sponsor here.

www.kinkismysuperpower.com

CONTENTS

Foreword	17
Introduction	19
Chiluna	28
Nate & K	32
Carol Queen	34
Jason	40
Mantis	44
Bondage Nexus	46
Stephan Ferris (aka Blue Bailey)	50
Race Bannon	54
Ellen	58
Daddypuss Rex	62
Lee Carl	64
Blue	66
Joseph Kindred	70
Julie Fennell	74
Beatrice Stonebanks	76
Christian Walters	80
SriSanjay	84
Margaret Cho	88
Lascare.O	92
Michael Hughes	94
Storm	98
Rio Spooner	102
Mystic Storm aka Sprite or Carrie	106
Caroline	Peter	110
Pegstress	114
Dave	118

*This book was a labor of love.
We dedicate it to all those who still must live in the shadows.*

PAGE	SUBJECT	COURTESY OF
303	Slush Puppy	Pride Unbound London
309	Zero	Sky Russell
315	Queen Cougar	Leland Carina
321	Tua	Contributor
325	Gudrun	Contributor
329	Johnny	Kegan Marling
331	Johnny	Jason Jackson
335	Graylin Thornton	Kegan Marling
339	Aspero	Patricia Kali. Model: Douce.
343	Susan Wright	Contributor
347	Liztli	Contributor
351	Spencer Bergstedt	Contributor
357	Penny	Yokai Lens
361	Nora	Contributor
367	Jay	Contributor

AFTERCARE

379	Race Bannon	Kristofer Weston
382	Patrick Davis	Contributor
385	Jörg Fockele	WooJin Lee
388	Lola De Milo	Contributor
392	Adam Ouderkirk	WooJin Lee
396	Beatrice Stonebanks	Lara George

PAGE	SUBJECT	COURTESY OF
163	Master Devyn Stone	Contributor
165	Master Devyn Stone	Contributor
169	Sky Russell	Contributor
173	Lady V	Contributor
179	Alistair LeatherHiraeth	Contributor
183	Rebecca	Sean	Joe Navas
187	Koki Vieto	Contributor
193	Jessamy Barker	Contributor
205	Catasta Charisma	Contributor
209	Felicity Azura	Contributor
217	Riptide	Contributor
221	Lola	Contributor
225	Karan Ma'am	Contributor
229	Tyger Yoshi / Tyger's Slave	Taco D Smit
237	Coco	Contributor
245	Ruby Ryder	Contributor
251	Fennec Fortune	Contributor
255	Ayzad	Alessandro Branca
259	Janet W. Hardy	Jenn Spain Photography
267	Inanna Justice	JinkLab
269	Inanna Justice	JinkLab
273	Flicker	Contributor
279	HiThereCatSuit	Contributor
283	Nunca	Sherpa00786
289	Sir Ivan	Ryan Coit
285	JimJam	Contributor

PHOTOGRAPHY CREDITS

PAGE	SUBJECT	COURTESY OF
16	Foreword | Margaret Cho	Sergio Garcia
29	Chiluna	Contributor
35	Carol Queen	Tristan Crane
41	Jason	Sir Diesel
47	Bondage Nexus	JTolandPhoto. Model: RopeSiren.
51	Stephan Ferris	Mike Ruiz
55	Race Bannon	Kristofer Weston
67	Blue	Contributor
77	Beatrice Stonebanks	Awagami fotografix
81	Christian Walters	Contributor
85	SriSanjay	Cortney Mansanarez
89	Margaret Cho	Sergio Garcia
95	Michael Hughes	Ryan Coit
99	Storm	Contributor
107	Mystic Storm	Ed Anderson
111	Caroline | Peter	Contributors
123	Sakura	Contributor
129	Gaz	Contributor
131	Gaz	Contributor
135	Master Kayne | Bambi	Contributor
141	Dolly	Elizabeth Grace Richards
143	Alexander Cheves	Jason Holland
151	Caritia	Mamana Karada
153	Caritia	Rene de Sans
155	Caritia	Rene de Sans. Model: Bishop Black
157	Río	Contributor

Our publisher and the team at Unbound Edition Press supported, guided, coordinated, and beautifully edited this book into the expansive expression of the kink communities it portrays — thank you. We especially appreciate the contributions of Cory Firestine, Joe Floresca, and Eleanor Safe.

To everyone who helped this project in any way, whether mentioned here or not, please know we are forever grateful that you allowed us to continue developing our documentary film project while also gracing us with the opportunity to create the unanticipated book you are now reading.

We thank each and every person we interviewed for the generosity, transparency, honesty, and vulnerability you shared with us, whether your story made it into the book or not. This book would quite literally not have happened without all of your contributions.

Speaking out or supporting those who do is so important because it lowers the perceived risk for those who remain silent for whatever reasons they deem necessary. To everyone involved in any way, your courage matters. Your words matter. Every voice is a key to empowering another's voice, and that's how liberation and freedom happen.

As we bring this book to a close, we express our deepest gratitude to each and every one of you who has supported us on this journey. Your love, encouragement, and counsel have meant the world to us, and we are forever grateful. To our loved ones who have stood by our side through late nights and early mornings, through laughter and tears, thank you for your unwavering support. To our community leaders and sponsors who have believed in us and our message, thank you for your generosity and trust. And to our advisors and mentors who have shared their wisdom and expertise with us, thank you for your guidance and direction. And importantly, since our bonds and friendship have grown so strong during the creation process, we each thank our fellow members of the team. Thank you for being a source of inspiration, motivation, joy, and strength. This book would not have been possible without all of us remaining cohesive and focused.

We are honored to share this book with the world.

promotion. Mister B, Nelson Sousa da Cunha Pochet, and RoB Berlin supported our international advisors' travels to San Francisco, and with additional donations to our project.

Special thanks go to the Society of Janus for their incredibly generous donation to and administrative sponsorship for the Divine Deviance film project. Their 50 years of trailblazing a safe, sane, and consensual pathway for kinksters is not only applauded but celebrated with deep appreciation and admiration. Without the daring bravery of those who came before us, and the unwavering support of those who continue to stand by our side, this book and our documentary film project wouldn't be possible.

Organizations and businesses across the kink and sex-positive spectrum provided sponsor support and helped publicize our fundraising efforts. These include SMart-Rhein-Ruhr e.V., Mister B, Good Vibrations, National Coalition for Sexual Freedom, Onyx, The Leather Journal, Grass Roots Gay Rights Foundation, The Alternative Sexualities Health Research Alliance, Richard Sprott, Ph.D., Kink.com, The 15 Association, Brian Kent, Cleveland Leather Annual Weekend, CineKink, Tom of Finland Foundation, Eufory, National Leather Association-International, Leatherati, KFSTV, Permission4Pleasure, Folsom Street, IG-BDSM, Libertine - Vienna, NachtSchatten, Porn Film Festival Berlin, Schmacht, SklavenZentrale.com, SMJG, SM News, and Strafbuch.

During the early gestation stage of the project, Caritia, Tobi Tentakel, Morgana Muses, and Vladi honored us with their knowledge, insights, and experience as advisors. Atelier. Vladi donated logo and graphic design support to our fledgling group.

The Center for Independent Documentary, our non-profit financial sponsor, has allowed us the ability to more easily raise money through the years of work on the film project, and the freedom to create this book.

ACKNOWLEDGEMENTS

To our friends, families, supporters, and communities,

We want to thank those who helped and supported us to bring this book into the world.

Our team has an abundance of people, businesses, and organizations to thank. So many have championed this book and the associated documentary film series thus far. As we express our thanks for a project spanning years in time, it's inevitable we're going to miss someone. We apologize in advance if we do.

All of us acknowledge our loved ones and families who uplifted our spirits, offered support through tough times and missed dinners, and listened to our ongoing ideas and hopes, and continue to do so.

When our documentary project first launched, certain people and organizations showed their faith with their donations and promotional outreach. There were also countless $5, $10, or $50 donations from all the individual donors who supported us at our initial fundraiser and over the years. Please know we're incredibly grateful for your faith in us and our project.

We thank Margaret Cho for not only writing the foreword to this book, but also for wholeheartedly believing in the project and lending us her considerable clout. Certain kink community members blessed us with their time and networks to help launch and sustain the project.

Early supporters we deeply thank are Midori, Graylin Thornton, Matthias T J Grimme, Carol Queen, Mufasa Ali, Rostom Mesli, Carol Queen, Peter Tupper, Rob Bienvenue, Gayle Rubin, Nelson Sousa da Cunha Pochet, Koki Vieto, Audrey Joseph, Cleo Dubois, Ray Tilton, and Peter Fiske.

Among early donors, Mr. S Leather donated a considerable amount to fund our initial project trailer which helped us kick off our efforts with high quality

Beatrice Stonebanks is an accomplished AI Business Strategist specializing in revenue generation. Renowned for her gender-nonconforming online global community, BoardroomDominatrix.com, Beatrice expertly navigates and scales both corporate and kink-adjacent domains. She is a five-time founder, an award-winning speaker, author, and community outreach leader. She develops, mentors, and launches start-up cohorts on an international scale. In 2024, she was inducted into the prestigious Society of Janus Hall of Fame.

I'm the same person I was before the project yet enriched with an invigorated layer — another gift from embracing kink. The transformative power of the human experience is unmatched, especially when it includes elements like kink that defy conventional norms. To truly understand, you must read the book, or better yet, experience kink for yourself and live it. I'm fortunate to be part of this team.

Having been involved with this project, I can truly say I feel seen, heard, celebrated, honored, cherished, loved, and accepted. What a ride it has been! I wouldn't trade a second of it for anything. The pure joy we shared supported us through incredibly challenging times, both globally and personally. It surprised me, my capacity to love a team that I mostly connected with via Zoom. We created spaces for tears, laughter, silliness, and celebrating every joy in each other's lives. It was a hoot! I will cherish this bond for all my years. Lovebombs abound on this team.

While the list of those to thank for this project could stretch into eternity for countless reasons, two stand out like radiant stars in the night sky. First, the Society of Janus, which has supported and empowered me to become the kinkster I am today. Second, my deepest thanks and heartfelt appreciation go to my partner, David, who turned my world upside down with his irresistible kink. David, thank you for the passion, fire, and unfathomable joy you bring to my every day.

BEATRICE STONEBANKS

The intention of the *Kink Is* project captured me immediately: a non-fiction depiction of kink simply didn't exist yet. It's right up my alley — nothing tops the thrill of real life. The high caliber of people already involved in the project assured me I could trust the outcome; I knew I needed to be a part of it.

When we began this endeavor, I proudly identified as a jaded motherfucker. This label wasn't derogatory to me; instead, it suggested someone who had navigated a few perverted blocks and knew the landscape so well that little could surprise them. The "motherfucker" aspect symbolized power — I was a kink-community leader, jaded yet in a position of influence, and I owned it with a smile. I particularly loved the smile, a defiance against the patriarchal expectation that a woman's worth increases with her pleasant demeanor. The type of authority I held — whether in a dungeon, my bedroom, or a boardroom — wasn't the kind that patriarchy finds comforting. My pronouns are She/Her/Sir. In the boardroom, men often cowered appropriately. In the kink community, people rallied by my side, grateful for the safe, sane, and consensual environment that matched the intensity of our craved play: kink, BDSM, and getting jiggy with our pink-bits.

Self-labeling as a jaded motherfucker made me stand out. Being a badass in business made my skills highly sought after. Contributing to my kinky community led me to join the Divine Deviance team, the collective behind our projects in books and films. I was eager to help fund an effort so significant; to show the uninitiated what I viewed as a profound gift — being kinky is an act of self-love.

After my usual business development tactics began to fizzle, I felt less potent within the team. Nevertheless, they supported me. Funding a film project was unlike anything I'd tackled before. My role expanded as we united in our mission to illuminate the joy and realities of kink and how it varies across different races, genders, ages, sexual identities, and desires.

Eight years later, our team is bound by a profound, eye-opening experience. None of us remain untouched by the scope, magnitude, and impact of interviewing hundreds of kinksters from various backgrounds. Exploration. Dignity. Wonder. Tantalizing. Dark.

Adam Ouderkirk has been an organizer and activist in the LGBTQ and HIV/STI service communities since 1981, expanding access to competent medical care and disease prevention, working toward freedom, equality, and sexual expression for all. In 20 years working in HIV care, he developed 30 new care and treatment sites, from initial research and design, through acquiring public funding, to staffing and program oversight. Adam's 40 years of design and program development experience — with the occasional dip into drag performance — has brought creativity and know-how to his involvement with non-profit filmmaking, and an ongoing devotion to alternative explorations.

about protecting their equipment from the splashes! Meeting people from all over the country and the world, and doing the interviews, I've been turned on, touched, saddened, gladdened, laughed out loud, and learned new ways of being human.

I didn't think of kink play as emotional before we started on the journey on this book and film project. I've learned that there is such an intense connection. There's such an emotional charge that happens when people allow themselves to play exactly how they want to play, say what they want, and get it. They're not thinking about where they are or who they are. They're just in the moment. To see that emotional connection and ecstatic communication, it's almost like two spirits are no longer separate; they're together. It's amazing. That alone is a reason to explore this kinky world, to be curious about it. So much of life is about trying to get something, trying to communicate something, trying to have someone hear. I love kink because the communication, when it's done right, happens really straightforwardly and aboveboard. Then you get to that moment where two people are getting exactly what they want. And it's magic.

What I've seen over and over and over, even in the most intense scenes where everyone has a serious face, or they're flogging the hell out of someone, is joy. There's this transformational joy that's happening. There's a freedom in that and an approach to moving through the world that allows for laughter at and with oneself, joyfully. There was a time when I couldn't access my own joy too much. Now I think of joy all the time. There is such joy in kinky play and kink community.

ADAM OUDERKIRK

The friendly acceptance and non-judgmental openness of the kink events and bars always intrigued and attracted me. Too many people see kinksters as "other" or "unknown" or "weird." The heart, love, and strength shown by the leather community's response to the AIDS crisis made me want a more honest and accurate depiction of kink and kinksters. This project has been an opportunity to harness my creative background and passion for people, and to show the truth *about* the community, *from* the community, *by* the community.

I've always loved non-traditional and creative people and situations — with an arts degree and background, a long career in the HIV/AIDS care and prevention field, drag/drag-adjacent much of my life, and sexually adventurous. I've seen myself as a non-kinkster who occasionally "dabbled," since leather, uniforms and tall boots, especially riding boots, have always held a fascination for me.

Eight or nine years into this, I can't say I'm necessarily any kinkier, but I've heard about more, and more varied, kinks than I ever thought possible — shared with stark honesty, gracious humility, and wild sexiness — and surrounded by joy, deep exploration, caring, kind humor, supportive strength, and a deep love for other human beings' humanity. I've been constantly reminded that everyone has a story and a journey, and that both will confound any assumptions our society expects of them. Understanding informed consent and continuous consent has transformed my view of the world and how to more completely respect others. If this is what a person wants or needs, if this is who a person says they are, I'm going to take it as that's who they are. I got it. It's not about me. Everyone can be whoever they want to be. Like that wonderful saying: Don't yuck someone else's yum.

Throughout this process, we've had moments of frustration, weeks of very hard work, months of setbacks and delays, some exhilarating highs, a fantastically wild and sexy fundraising party, and loads of laughs and some tears. In our production meetings, we'd have so much work to get done, and yet still have time to share funny, sexy stories, like the one about someone — who shall remain nameless here — being "accidentally fisted"! While filming the pee pool at the Folsom Street Fair, for our associated documentary film project, our (very vanilla) camera and sound crew were more concerned about getting the shot right than

Silke Niggemeier (Lola De Milo) is a systemic family therapist (IGST), systemic sex therapist (IFSEX, IGST) NLP coach (DVNLP), mediator, BDSM activist, educator and multimedia artist, former long-standing member on the board of the oldest registered association for kinksters in Germany/Europe (SMart-Rhein-Ruhr e.V.) and former board member of the German Society for Social Scientific Sexual Research (DGSS) 30+ years of kink experience, public speaking, event organizing and her general interest in how humans function and love, brought her to *Kink Is*. Silke Niggemeier coined the terms Consensual Emotional Voyeurism (CEV) and Emotional Voyeurism (EV) and published on this subject internationally.

I personally went through deep crisis when I realized how far Covid and moving to another country had taken me away from my kink identity and community and how much healing I still had to do after the outing. I was given the time and opportunity I needed by this wonderful group of open-minded and open-hearted people for which I am immensely grateful.

Kink Is is a love letter to humans who dare to be themselves. To you, the reader, and also to us who were fortunate to be trusted with these glimpses into dungeons, bedrooms, and hearts.

I am hopeful that Kink Is can illuminate a part of humanity that is still so often undeservedly feared. I celebrate Kink Is as I celebrate my survival. And I hope this book helps all those out in the world who are living in doubt and fear about what turns on themselves or their loved ones.

Behind the scenes there was laughter, dirty jokes, passionate discussions, and coffee. Lots of coffee! Sleepless nights, Friday Zooms, tears of all kinds, frustrations, riling the troupes, hopes and wishes and dreams. Visits across continents. Braving fear of flying! Moments of awe and wonder.

"People trust us with this? We get to live and experience this? How lucky are we?!" Lots of swearing. And coffee! Believing in Kink Is when nobody did was hard, but never a chore. We had our own little rituals — hearts at the end of each Zoom call — that bound us together and got us through. This team is as varied, weird, and wonderful as they come.

We have a "jaded motherfucker" who is warm and emotional and astounded by moments of human connection. We have carers and givers and grammar Nazis and number crunchers. We have gifted writers and a director who sometimes calls us to order with a straight faced: "Kids!" and also converted me to oat milk. Oh, and there were plenty of lube jokes ...

My heartfelt thanks:
To my weird nerdy vanilla man for his nurturing care and support and questions!
To my first Top Dave and all the subs that followed.
To Ulrich Clement in Heidelberg for his precise teachings and ability to embrace kink into the curriculum.
To Matthias T.J. Grimme for introducing me to Divine Deviance.
To all my clients and students for their curiosity and inquisitiveness.
And last, but not least to H., P. (Kell) & O. Ich hab euch lieb.

SILKE NIGGEMEIER / LOLA DE MILO

When I was asked to join this project, I was a mental health professional, a mother, a well-connected and busy BDSM activist in leadership positions, a survivor of public outing and shaming, a woman with history. As a woman, especially a mother, you are still easily targeted if you have anything remotely to do with sex outside the socially sanctioned norm. I am a sex coach; a family therapist and I live BDSM/Kink and poly.

This is what happened to me in 2012: A man whose advances I refused, abused his power in the local community to publicly out me. I lost almost everything at that point. I had the choice to hide in shame or work as hard as I could so this wouldn't happen to anybody else! Nobody should lose their life, their self, and their dignity over the way they love.

In June 2016 I got a call from a wonderful friend, the German Bondage Master, author and Owner of Germany's longest running BDSM magazine, Matthias T. J. Grimme.

His words: "Hey, there is this guy in San Francisco who contacted us. He needs info and contacts for his film project. Are you interested?"

Of course I was!

After contacting Jörg Fockele and learning about Divine Deviance, a creative collective taking form, I burned for the project and fell in love with the people. I was hoping to be able to watch this grow and get out into the world. I remember being super excited and getting up in the middle of the night to read my emails. The 9-hour time difference between SFO and PAD flipped my world around a little, but I didn't care. I wanted this with all my heart. I wanted something that I could proudly slam in the faces of those who had shamed me and say: *This is my truth and I AM NOT ALONE!* That's why I almost burst with excitement when I received the invitation to be part of the team! It's really hard to not use F-words to describe my joy! I cried happy tears. Still do while I am writing this.

In no other professional context have I ever been so safe or welcome to be me. We all put on our masks when we go out into the world. Most even the fighting gloves, the gauntlets, the emotional padding. That's not the case in this team.

Kink Is lives from emotional availability, from years and years of showing up and checking in with each other. Through weddings and funerals, babies and depression, private and professional triumphs, health scares and retirement. Kink Is is possible because all of us believed in the value of people's stories, their lives and loves, struggles and joys!

Jörg Fockele is an award-winning filmmaker, producer and TV director with a career spanning 30 years. He has written and/or directed five feature documentaries, 10+ short films, and numerous music videos and PSAs. His television credits include Bravo's *Queer Eye,* ABC's *Wife Swap,* MTV's *Savage U,* and AMC's *Small Town Security*.

JÖRG FOCKELE

Full disclosure right up front: I'm as vanilla as they come. I'd been to a few Folsom Street Fairs (fully clothed) and directed and produced a few short projects about the kink community prior to my involvement in this book adventure. But that was the extent of my connection. I do realize that control, having control, giving up control in any context (sexual, emotional, professional) holds a fascination for me. But as much as I adore my kinkster friends, I would feel like a fraud claiming kinkster status for myself. But then again: Where is the demarcation line between kinky and vanilla? And who decides? And does that line even exist, or don't we all live on a spectrum just like we do with most things?

If I remember it correctly, I was one of the initial creators of the project — that was actually late 2015 (and I have the email threads to prove it.) I had done a couple of video projects as a director with the kink community in San Francisco and really fallen in love with the people. I reached out to our co-author Race Bannon (among a couple of other kinksters), to see what he thought of the idea of creating a series of "modular" online short films about the kink community. Over the course of the years, the project morphed from there, via attempts to turn it into a television series with Margaret Cho and into the book you are reading right now. The film project is still in the works.

Eight years of (unpaid) collaboration later I am still as vanilla as I was in 2015. I do have a better understanding of what kink is and I have certainly learned a thing or two about consent (in any context for that matter) and about boundaries. And I consider those gifts. I strongly believe that kinksters' ability to negotiate consent and their siblinghood have a lot to teach vanilla folks. But that aside, I wouldn't have spent all these years trying to push the project forward and making it past many doors slammed in our faces if it wasn't for the amazing group of individuals who are Divine Deviance, the collective behind *Kink Is*. We never gave up and we supported and carried each other when one of us was losing faith or going through a rough spot. But most importantly in all of our weekly (!) meetings since 2016 we got shit done and we laughed our asses off. I'm beyond excited that all of our hard work paid off and took on the shape of this beautiful book. I will also really miss our Friday morning sessions!

Patrick Davis is an accomplished author, critic, entrepreneur, and publisher. He leads Unbound Edition Press, a literary publishing house he founded to advance work from overlooked, underappreciated, or marginalized authors; its titles have earned widespread critical acclaim and multiple bestseller rankings. He is a voting member of the National Book Critics Circle. His most recent writing is featured in *Harvard Review, Kenyon Review, Gertrude, Great River Review, Provincetown Arts, Salamander,* and *Rain Taxi Review of Books,* among other notable journals. Additionally, he has ghost-written six books for the world's major publishers. He conducted his graduate research in American literature at Washington University in St. Louis. Mr. Davis founded and served as executive director of the world's first anti-bullying fund, supporting LGBTQ+ projects across the U.S and the U.K.

I was officially declared disabled. I did not have a sexual pulse — or a single orgasm — for more than six years. I barely made it through alive. Death would have been welcome relief.

Books had always saved my life during its hardest passages and starting Unbound Edition Press proved to be the healing salve I needed. It was the fearlessness of our own literary dissenters who showed me how to find and express my own authenticity. Deeply dedicated and loving people helped return me to some degree of health, to my own body, and its long-denied joys. What came next surprised me: I found incredible power, agency, and self-possession through safe, sane, and consensual explorations of kink. It had never occurred to me that this would be part of my healing path.

Through kink, I regained control of my own body, commanding for myself — and for the first time — how pain and pleasure alike could intersect and balance out what had for so long been inaccessible to me. I became free, authentic, unafraid … fearless.

For me, the entwinement of kink and a literary project has felt like a completeness, finally, and yet one without end. A completeness that can only become more complete as I join voices with others who have had both similar and totally different experiences from my own.

What I know with certainty is that this book would not have been possible without my own challenges and triumphs, or without those of every human represented here. In my experience and view, *Kink Is* … heroic, a victory, a dissent from how things could have been. I hope this book might do some similarly powerful work in your life, too.

PATRICK DAVIS

I came to this project belatedly, just as I did to my own authentic sexuality. The Divine Deviance collective had been at work on the concept for how to tell, honor, and de-stigmatize the true stories of kinky people for several years. I entered into this dedicated and passionate group of complex thinkers, media makers, and kink practitioners with the intent to help jump-start the documentary film side of the multi-media project. We faced unexpected obstacles on that part of our journey (though it is very much moving forward) and decided my most immediate contributions could come through my work as a publisher.

Unbound Edition Press was already well-known for several bestselling memoirs and monographs on non-traditional sexualities and genders. I brought with me our press mission: to publish literary dissent from fearless authors. The Divine Deviance collective fit perfectly with that, and so we decided to make a book filled with other dissenting stories from other fearless people. That book became *Kink Is*.

Finding my way here, though, required me to be fearless, too — vulnerable, honest, courageous. I came of age in the darkest shadows of the AIDS plague in the 80s and 90s — and buried 19 friends before I turned 30. My childhood was defined by denial, shame, hiding, and religious and family trauma. I hid myself to survive. I spent my 20s safely nose-down in books during my nearly decade-long (and practically celibate) graduate studies. I buried myself in an overwhelming and damaging cycle of work addiction throughout my 30s and into my 40s. I was assuredly a gay man through it all, if largely in name only, but I was not a full person. I was disconnected from myself, my body, and my community.

As I approached 50, I was hit with a truly unbelievable series of medical diagnoses: On top of my lifelong Type 1 Diabetes, I gained the burden of an extraordinarily rare combination of autoimmune, neurological, and muscular disorders. Multiple Sclerosis. Chronic Inflammatory Demyelinating Polyneuropathy. Stiff Persons Syndrome. I was fighting myself – my own body and being — from the inside out. Then, a devastatingly botched surgical procedure left me in what I can still describe only as suicidal pain. My body and life collapsed.

Race Bannon has been an organizer, writer, publisher, educator, commentator, leader, speaker, and activist in the LGBTQ, leather/kink, polyamory, and HIV/STI prevention realms since 1973. He is an author, widely published writer, active speaker, community organizer and project leader, and has received numerous national and local awards. He's also a regular cast member of the online series, *On Guard Cigar Salon*. You can find links to Race's writings and projects on his social media profiles which exist on all major platforms.

RACE BANNON

After working with one of our team members, Jörg Fockele, on a documentary project as one of the interview subjects, I immediately recognized Jörg as someone of deep curiosity, integrity, and talent. That project was undertaken by the National AIDS Memorial Grove to recognize the contributions of the San Francisco leather community during the worst of the AIDS crisis. That interview and overall experience was so beautiful and sensitively handled that when Jörg floated the idea to expand on the topic of kink sexuality and its communities that had piqued his interest, I didn't hesitate to jump onboard.

At that time, when our team first embarked on the original Divine Deviance documentary project, I was a different person than I am today. My perspectives were narrower. My mind was more closed. My depth of understanding of kinksters and kink communities was vast, but not nearly as comprehensive as it is now.

Sure, I had a long history within the leather and kink scenes. As I write this, I've been active in the leather, kink, fetish, or whatever one chooses to call this type of adventurous sexuality so many enjoy and commune around, for 52 years. Even with that robust baseline of information and experience, this *Kink Is* project has expanded my understanding and horizons beyond expectations.

When this book began to take shape after countless meetings and a multitude of interviews, I stepped back and realized I had changed so much. How I viewed kink and those who live it changed. Each person interviewed seemed to add another layer or aspect to what I had previously believed I fully understood. Clearly, I did not. I thank each person interviewed for educating me in ways that I hope this book will now educate others.

Working on this project has been pure joy. Joy working with an incredible authoring team. Joy working with a publisher who respects kinksters, our communities, and our culture. Joy interacting with the interview subjects who represent a wide swath of kinksters and the communities in which they navigate.

I hope you, the reader, can feel the palpable joy I felt through the words and images herein. If kink has a baseline emotion, for me it's joy. May that joy positively inform your own sexuality and relationships whether you partake personally or simply revel as a bystander of a collection of human beings who have found passion, connection, and meaning in this particular way of celebrating the erotic.

Then digest what you read and saw ...

> How do I feel?
> Where do I feel it?
> What did I learn?
> Who did I relate to most?
> Why did certain things intrigue me ... or not?
> What or whom do I understand better now?
> Where do I want to go from here?

These are some of the kinds of questions that might come up naturally. Check in again with your feelings and thoughts a few days later, too. Exploring this with yourself or a person you shared this book with is an extension of the trust and safe exploration that is possible in aftercare.

Some kinksters consensually decide to do this alone or not at all. That is okay, too.

No matter what your answers — or questions — may be, know that we've been present and here with you the entire time.

Who are we?

Just read on for insights on your *Kink Is* care team: the interviewers, transcribers, collectors, curators, writers, and editors.

AFTERCARE

Throughout this book, you may have noticed the mention of "aftercare" in some personal stories. This refers to the moments after a kink scene has concluded, when the participants take intentional time to check-in, connect, nourish, communicate, and "come down" together. Aftercare is when kinksters reaffirm each other, validate what they each experienced, and provide some comfort.

It serves as a bridge back to reality and everyday life, rounding out the experience. Whether the participants are physically or emotionally close, or part ways afterward, aftercare provides the service of storing the harvested emotions and sensations so they may be transformed into energy to brave the world.

Aftercare is an essential part of a Kink/BDSM encounter.

Most of the time, something pretty intense has just happened and a moment to breathe together and appreciate each other is both smart and rewarding.

Tops and bottoms, subs and doms, all deserve aftercare. Everyone involved has been vulnerable, extended trust, explored some chosen headspace, shared their body, and put in a lot of energy to create a shared experience. In the dreamlike or hyper-focused state of connectedness after a scene, it feels extra safe to hear, "I was with you the entire time."

In reading *Kink Is,* you have been led on a roller coaster of emotions and experiences, even if vicariously. The stories and images, the ideas and perspectives shared here may take some time to process.

We invite you to do this in typical aftercare fashion: maybe get comfortable in a tranquil, quiet space, have a nice snack and a beverage, make sure you are cared for.

In reading this book, you've been a voyeur.
And that's a bit ...

KINKY.

For me personally, kink is an orientation. It's this association with pleasure and pain. For me it doesn't have to do with power dynamics or role playing or humiliation or any of that. So that's how I define it for me. I understand that word as much broader. It means a lot of things to a lot of people. A lot of times it means sexuality outside the mainstream. Sometimes it's about a spiritual pursuit. It's about getting to know your limits, getting to know yourself, intimacy with the people that you're practicing with, that you're sharing with. It's all those things. There's diversity to be had because for all the people you ask what that definition is, you're probably gonna get twice that number of answers about what kink is.

As far as what turns me on, what brings me sexual joy? What are my fantasies? What do I get off on? I'm not gonna answer that. This is highly personal and none of your business. My answer to anyone who asks is: *That really is private.*

FRANCINE

PRONOUNS	She/They	**RELATIONSHIP STATUS OR STRUCTURE**	Monogamous
GENDER IDENTITY	Demi-nonbinary	**AGE**	52
SEXUAL ORIENTATION	Queer	**LOCATION**	Midwest, U.S.

AS FAR AS WHAT TURNS ME ON, WHAT BRINGS ME SEXUAL JOY? WHAT ARE MY FANTASIES? WHAT DO I GET OFF ON? I'M NOT GONNA ANSWER THAT. THIS IS HIGHLY PERSONAL AND **NONE OF YOUR BUSINESS.** MY ANSWER TO ANYONE WHO ASKS IS: *THAT REALLY IS PRIVATE.*

Kink has intentionally been non-sexual for me most of the time. Kink is deeply connected to trust and intimacy, whether emotional or physical. Intimacy does not have to be synonymous with sex for me.

x x x

Pain is different from harm. Being a masochist in a kinky sense, particularly for me in a non-sexual sense, is not that different than people who seek thrills in other ways, whether that's roller coasters, or horror movies, or getting tattooed. These people would not necessarily identify as masochists, but I would argue that those are physically intense experiences that are not that different from non-sexual kink at the core of it. And when I phrase it that way, people get it. So that has been something that I have found important to explain to people even within the kink world, because so many kinky people don't understand that you can play non-sexually.

> Kink is deeply connected to trust and intimacy, whether emotional or physical. Intimacy does not have to be synonymous with sex

PEPPER

PRONOUNS	▇▇▇▇▇▇	RELATIONSHIP STATUS OR STRUCTURE	▇▇▇▇▇▇
GENDER IDENTITY	Woman+	AGE	30
SEXUAL ORIENTATION	Bisexual/Pansexual	LOCATION	San Francisco, U.S.

PAIN IS DIFFERENT FROM HARM.

I've often pondered why it seems that trans people are over-represented in the kink community. I did get one flattering answer from a friend of mine: Since trans people have to really do a lot of self-examination and, and in most cases, make some radical changes in their lives, they've done the work to accept themselves that cis people often haven't. But, that rings false to me. I think in our brains, that kink, gender identity, and sexual orientation are connected. They are "neighbors," somehow. Kink and gender identity and sexual orientation seem to develop right around the same age.

x x x

The first time I was at the Folsom Street Fair, I went to a play party, thrown by the Exiles (the women's BDSM org). I met another trans woman who did some pretty mean things to me. She tickled me, which I loved. And put me all the way on the floor and stomped on my butt wearing Doc Martens, and it was the biggest endorphin rush I have ever had in my life. It was a peak experience for me, and it was icing on the cake that I had this epic kinky experience, courtesy of a woman who's a lot like me!

x x x

There are a few things I'd like non-kinksters to know. I want to describe why I love impact play, because getting hit in the back with a flogger may seem totally incomprehensible to some people. *How that could be pleasant in any way?* Once the endorphins start going, what it's like for me is it kind of sneaks up on me. I'm getting hit and I can sort of take each moment as it comes and just let it go. It begins to feel like I've often heard meditation described, a similar state of mind, perhaps. You're getting high on your own brain chemicals.

MAURA

PRONOUNS	She/Her	RELATIONSHIP STATUS OR STRUCTURE	Single
GENDER IDENTITY	Woman	AGE	56
SEXUAL ORIENTATION	Lesbian	LOCATION	Seattle, U.S.

IT BEGINS TO FEEL LIKE I'VE OFTEN HEARD **MEDITATION** DESCRIBED, A SIMILAR STATE OF MIND, PERHAPS. YOU'RE GETTING HIGH ON YOUR OWN BRAIN CHEMICALS.

JAY

PRONOUNS	He/Him	**RELATIONSHIP STATUS OR STRUCTURE**	Married, Polyamorous
GENDER IDENTITY	Cis Man	**AGE**	60
SEXUAL ORIENTATION	Gay	**LOCATION**	Vermont, U.S.

> There's a lot of shame around sex, and that can be hot. Shame can be hot and you can play with shame.

I grew up in New England, two hours south of Montreal, but Boston was founded by Puritans and never recovered. The sexual culture in New England is very different than the sexual culture in San Francisco. There's a lot of shame around sex, and that can be hot. Shame can be hot and you can play with shame. But it's not the way I like to live in my day-to-day existence.

One day, I wore a leather-studded belt to work because I was going to be leaving from there to go to a gay campground, I wore my campground clothes, thinking I was going to be in my office alone and no one would see me. But I forgot there was a company lunch. So as I'm standing in line at it, one of my coworker friends was behind me. He looks at me and says, "Shouldn't that say big fister?" That's when I realized that I was wearing my leather-studded belt that said "pig fister" on it.

x x x

Transgression is hot. That was really challenging for me when I was younger. I was raised as a pacifist, but I liked hurting people. Hurting men. Hurting guys. Not random ones, but ones that I cared for, who cared for me. It was really hard for me to reconcile those two parts of me for a long time.

Pacifism is not using violence to solve problems, right? That's different than consensual violence. There is a difference there. I didn't understand it when I was younger, having these feelings and trying to figure them out. If it's consensual, it's not really violence. I talk about this when I'm fisting, but it applies to lots of other activities. Like, it's not pain. It's intensity. I frame pain as when my body is being irrevocably damaged. Everything else is just intensity. You can master intensity. I think it was realizing that there's this split between non-consensual violence and then these things that look like violence but when they're consensual they're something else completely.

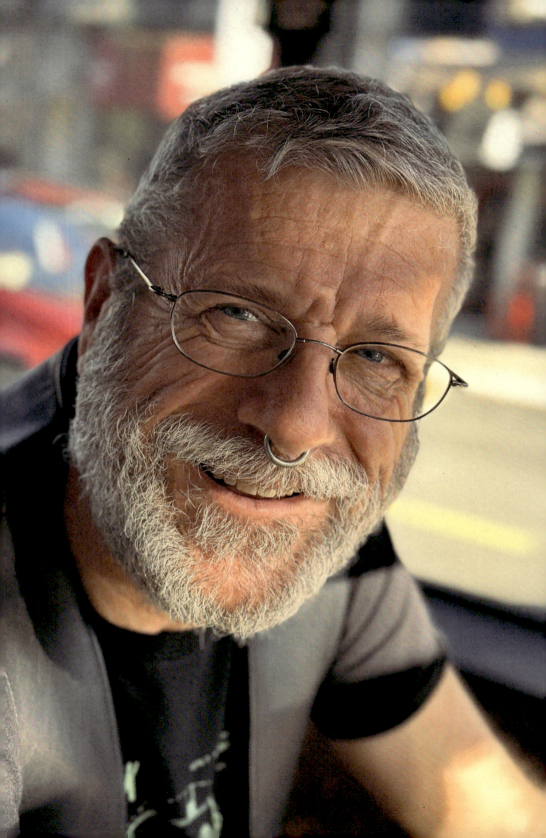

IF IT'S CONSENSUAL, IT'S NOT REALLY VIOLENCE.

LIKE, IT'S NOT PAIN. IT'S INTENSITY. I FRAME PAIN AS WHEN MY BODY IS BEING IRREVOCABLY DAMAGED. EVERYTHING ELSE IS JUST INTENSITY. YOU CAN MASTER INTENSITY.

People will ask, "What are you into?" I always say, "What am I not into? That's the shorter list." But my favorite kink would be worship. Being worshiped, being put on that pedestal, knowing you mean something to someone in such a deep, meaningful, connected way. Even if they don't understand you as a person, they find value in you, and who you are — so, not just physical worship, but emotional worship. I think that's really powerful. It can be extremely intimate.

    It's generally foot or hand worship: them kneeling, me seated or standing. That supplicating pose of kneeling on the floor and looking up at the person that they're worshiping with those eyes of adoration. The expression that we share, not just him to me, but me to him. That connection and love is something that I would love to share with others.

NORA

PRONOUNS	They/Them	**RELATIONSHIP STATUS OR STRUCTURE**	▇▇▇▇▇
GENDER IDENTITY	Non-Binary	**AGE**	▇▇▇▇▇
SEXUAL ORIENTATION	Pansexual	**LOCATION**	Los Angeles, U.S.

EVEN IF THEY DON'T UNDERSTAND YOU AS A PERSON, THEY **FIND VALUE** IN YOU, AND WHO YOU ARE — SO, **NOT JUST PHYSICAL WORSHIP, BUT EMOTIONAL WORSHIP.** I THINK THAT'S REALLY POWERFUL. IT CAN BE **EXTREMELY INTIMATE.**

I had big issues accepting the BDSM side of myself. I knew it was there but I just didn't want to accept it. At that point I was already married in a "vanilla" marriage. And it was kind of weird for me that I had everything that I was supposed to have, meaning, I had my husband, my apartment, my job. I had checked those tick boxes that society had told me I was supposed to have checked at this age. And I was like, *Okay, now everyone is happy. Can I now be happy? Can I now decide what I want to do with the rest of my life?* It kind of felt like that, for me at least. And that's when I said, *Okay, I'm ready. Everything is in order. Now I can do this.* And that's when I started my kink journey. Today, I am very active member, educator, and lead organizer in my local community and my vanilla marriage turned into a happy polyamorous marriage.

x x x

I have fibromyalgia, a condition that's described as a fatigue syndrome with widespread pain. When I practice BDSM activities, kink activities, it allows me to not feel that pain because my brain is either really relaxed or dealing with another type of pain. It's no longer concentrating on the fibromyalgia pain. It's not therapy, but it helps with processing pain in the long-term. It's almost like a puzzle. It's like trying to reconnect with my body in a sense. Due to fibromyalgia my body reacts differently to certain stimuli or certain kinks. Sometimes it feels like resistance training, both mentally and physically.

PENNY

PRONOUNS	She/Her	**RELATIONSHIP STATUS OR STRUCTURE**	Polyamorous
GENDER IDENTITY	Cis Female	**AGE**	▇▇▇
SEXUAL ORIENTATION	Queer	**LOCATION**	Paris, France

IT'S NOT THERAPY, BUT IT HELPS WITH PROCESSING PAIN IN THE LONG-TERM. IT'S ALMOST **LIKE A PUZZLE.** IT'S LIKE **TRYING TO RECONNECT WITH MY BODY** IN A SENSE.

creates fear about those of us who are queer, trans, or kinky, is that we've had to look at those questions. And that makes us know things in a way that others don't. When you do have to take those kinds of deep dives, you develop a different sensibility. You have wisdom, you have knowledge that they're not privy to. That knowledge, I think, is what scares them.

SPENCER BERGSTEDT

PRONOUNS	He/Him	**RELATIONSHIP STATUS OR STRUCTURE**	Polyamorous with one primary partner and one D/s dynamic
GENDER IDENTITY	Man/Trans Man	**AGE**	61
SEXUAL ORIENTATION	Queer	**LOCATION**	Greater Seattle Area, U.S.

that people do and the folks who I tend to see embrace kink more as a definer of who they are, tend to be cisgender, heterosexual people with whom I might have nothing in common. I'm a leatherman 24/7. It doesn't matter whether I'm engaging in kink or not. That's just the physical thing that I might be doing.

With that being said, when I found a leather community, what I found was a group of people who were absolutely willing to celebrate my masculinity in a way that I had not found outside of that. And so there was never a question within the leather community that people called me Sir. Or that people called me Daddy. It didn't matter what my assigned sex at birth was; it didn't matter how I might have to live my life legally. They simply saw me as male-identified. It was a really welcoming and safe place for me to be myself. When I did decide to undergo physical transition, that was the community that was fully embracing right from the start.

x x x

Probably the most important thing that I think non-kinky people can learn from kinky people — like what straight people can learn from queer people — is a degree of self-examination. I don't think non-kinky people or straight people typically engage in that as deeply. One of the things about being queer, or about being transgender, or about being kinky, is that you really have to take a deep dive into yourself. *Who am I? What are my motivations? Why am I attracted to this? How is that going to work for me in my day-to-day life? How does that inform how I function in society? How does this impact my political choices, my social choices, my friendship choices, the work that I do?*

I don't think that straight people or cis people or non-kinky people ever have to ask any of those questions of themselves. So, sometimes I think the thing that

> Probably the most important thing that I think non-kinky people can learn from kinky people — like what straight people can learn from queer people — is a degree of self-examination.

My interest in kink started when I was a little kid. It fell into the categories of things like really enjoying playing with friends, and then doing things like interrogation scenes. But I have one really strong memory of physically inflicting pain on somebody. I was really enjoying it, and I was about probably seven or eight. I was playing with my best friend who lived across the street, and we were playing with Hot Wheels, which used this bright orange track that had little raised edges along the sides. And he whacked me in the leg with a piece of it. I was not happy about that. And so, I went home. And a little while later he came over and apologized and he said, "Well, you can hit me back." And I did. I hit him with it. And it left these nice little parallel marks on his leg. There was something about that. It was very visceral for me.

In kink, for me, there's not just the physical rush of it, though there's certainly that element of having your adrenaline running. It's a little bit like people who do extreme sports. Part of why you do it is to get that adrenaline rush, that endorphin high. But more so than that, I think there's something just deeply satisfying on an emotional and intellectual level, at a spiritual level, about having the kind of connection that you have with another human being when you're exploring the limits of physical endurance, physical pain. I do a lot of D/s too, and there's just the connection that comes with somebody who is choosing to give you the gift of their submission, there's an elegance in that and it's really beautiful. A lot of kink is that beauty in that grace. It's deep and it's meaningful.

x x x

I was assigned female at birth. And I've always been a very masculine-presenting person. I grew up in the 60s and 70s and there wasn't a lot of talk about trans people at that time. I knew that I was attracted to women. So, you know, the only default was that you identified as a lesbian, which didn't entirely fit but it was workable. There was a roadmap of how to interact. When I first came into kink, I was still identifying as a butch dyke. I was really in the leather community, and I separate that from the kink community. Leather is very rooted in queer culture and queer politics and queer dynamics. Kink, for me, is a descriptor of things

PART OF WHY YOU DO IT IS TO GET THAT ADRENALINE RUSH, THAT ENDORPHIN HIGH. BUT MORE SO THAN THAT, I THINK THERE'S SOMETHING JUST **DEEPLY SATISFYING** ON AN EMOTIONAL AND INTELLECTUAL LEVEL, AT A SPIRITUAL LEVEL, ABOUT HAVING THE KIND OF CONNECTION THAT YOU HAVE WITH ANOTHER HUMAN BEING WHEN YOU'RE EXPLORING THE LIMITS OF PHYSICAL ENDURANCE, PHYSICAL PAIN.

It's easy to say you must give consent for things to happen and that you must feel comfortable retracting consent — but it's much more difficult to actually do it. Non-kinksters could benefit from learning about consent, and the communication it requires. I found that many vanilla people do not want to communicate. They want what they want by giving subtle signals. But subtle signals don't work most of the time. I find it's much better to just talk about when you do or don't want to do something, rather than suffering in silence.

LIZTLI

PRONOUNS	He/They	**RELATIONSHIP STATUS OR STRUCTURE**	▓▓▓▓▓▓
GENDER IDENTITY	Non-Binary	**AGE**	25
SEXUAL ORIENTATION	Asexual	**LOCATION**	France

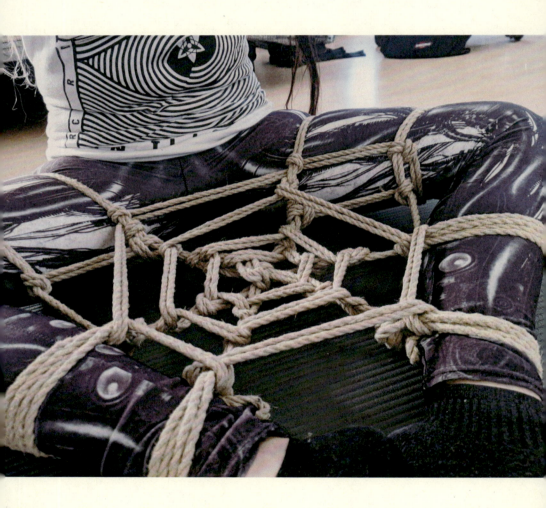

SUBTLE SIGNALS DON'T WORK MOST OF THE TIME.

LGBTQ+ communities changed and formed in new ways back in the 90s with individuals coming out to people that they knew. It was no longer *them*. Rather, it was: *Oh, that's my cousin. It's my brother. It's my uncle*. It was that personal coming out that made such a transformation in American society. But yet we can't really urge kinky people to come out because there's still discrimination. There's still stigma. We've only just decriminalized BDSM in the Model Penal Code on Sexual Assault. That's not even been published yet. Once it's published, then we can start lobbying states to adopt this legal framework for consent to kink. Having that and having the American Psychological Association depathologize kink, saying we are mentally healthy as a whole will hopefully combine to really lessen the stigma. I would love to see a time when people don't have to be afraid of being out as kinky.

SUSAN WRIGHT

PRONOUNS	She/Her	RELATIONSHIP STATUS OR STRUCTURE	Married, Polyamorous
GENDER IDENTITY	Female	AGE	60
SEXUAL ORIENTATION	Bisexual	LOCATION	Phoenix, Arizona, U.S.

Kink really impacts all of my life. When I first started exploring my sexuality, I realized I can set my own limits. I can tell somebody what it is that I want, and actually have a discussion about it, and control what's happening to my own body, and control my own journey. That has had huge payoffs in the rest of my life.

Sometimes I'm trying things out just to see how it makes me feel. I'm kind of a warrior at heart. So, a lot of what I really remember is from things I've seen. I've watched from before a scene starts all the way through to the end and afterwards, just to see that whole transition and the effects of it. Things I like being able to watch include the Dance of Souls, an event during which they dance with hooks pierced through their flesh. I could not do this for myself, because I have physical issues that prevent me from doing it. But when I had a very bad year and I needed some sort of catharsis, I thought, well, here's something that's happening. I want to experience this. So, I went to attend the Dance of Souls without actually participating, and I have to tell you I had the most intense experience just from being in that environment. They were invoking the spirits. Someone got up and invoked the Spirit of the West and said, "We welcome the darkness. We embrace the darkness and pass through it." I started crying. I must have cried for hours after that. Just watching and experiencing and feeling other people's own ecstatic journeys took me on my own. That really showed me there's a lot more happening here than just the physical. This is a whole body experience. I felt connected to everybody there in a way I just really hadn't expected because I wasn't even going there to participate. It was the community experience that helped make it so impactful.

> Just watching and experiencing and feeling other people's own ecstatic journeys took me on my own. That really showed me there's a lot more happening here than just the physical. This is a whole body experience.

x x x

I'M KIND OF A WARRIOR AT HEART.

Just before I left Paris to come back to Brazil, we had a play party, and I played with some rope with one of my partners. And she was really sensitive that day, so she just left the dungeon to take a seat in the lounge. She left, and I went after her, and we just sat there on the couch having some aftercare and talking and cuddling. Then slowly, bit by bit, some other people who had been playing started to come together. Initially, we were just two people sitting on the couch. And then, out of nowhere, we are a group of eight or nine people, all together and caring for each other. It was such a sweet, sweet moment. I remember really clearly that I could see the door to the dungeon, and the lounge was kind of dark with just some light coming from the dungeon door. I could hear the sounds of people getting whipped and moaning. It was so intimate, in so many different ways. It was a beautiful moment that happened out of someone being too sensitive to play. Yet sensitivity was transformed.

ASPERO

PRONOUNS	He/Him	**RELATIONSHIP STATUS OR STRUCTURE**	Married
GENDER IDENTITY	Man	**AGE**	40
SEXUAL ORIENTATION	Straight	**LOCATION**	São Paulo, Brazil

IT WAS A BEAUTIFUL MOMENT THAT HAPPENED OUT OF SOMEONE BEING TOO SENSITIVE TO PLAY. YET SENSITIVITY WAS TRANSFORMED.

When I think about who I am today and especially the legacy that I'm going to leave, I think about the other people in my life who've influenced me. I don't look at it as my legacy. It is their legacy.

Whenever I speak to younger people, especially people of color, I tell them who said what to me. I always say, Alan Selby said this to Vern Stewart who said to me: *None of this is about you*. And I say that to the younger people just so that they know that this isn't about them. It's not about any of us. It's about all of us.

Everything that I do reflects on everyone that I'm involved with. People look at me and they think, you know, I have something to contribute. But I'm only contributing what others contributed to me. The lessons that I learned from Tony Deblase, I pass those on. The things Midori has said to me, I pass those on. So I have no original ideas. They're all ideas from someone else. So my legacy, I believe, is to act as a bridge between the people that I knew then and the people I know now. I want to make sure the people who are in my life now know and understand that this has been going on forever and that they're part of something that's much, much bigger than themselves.

GRAYLIN THORNTON

PRONOUNS	He/Him/His	RELATIONSHIP STATUS OR STRUCTURE	Partnered
GENDER IDENTITY	Male	AGE	63
SEXUAL ORIENTATION	Gay	LOCATION	▮▮▮▮▮

I WANT TO MAKE SURE THE PEOPLE WHO ARE IN MY LIFE NOW KNOW AND UNDERSTAND THAT **THIS HAS BEEN GOING ON FOREVER** AND THAT THEY'RE PART OF SOMETHING THAT'S **MUCH, MUCH BIGGER** **THAN THEMSELVES.**

Kink, fundamentally, is trust. From there, it just expands into relationship building and community, romantic relationships, friendships, things like that. But kink is that building of trust with yourself, as well as building that trust with others in ways that, in order to be safe, force you to dig deeper and communicate and be uncomfortable. To get comfortable with being uncomfortable, whether that's physically, mentally, emotionally.

Kink makes me feel safe in a way that I never had in vanilla relationships or in workplaces even, or any types of other day-to-day vanilla dynamics. There is no gray area. Everything is clearly expressed, everything is negotiated. Boundaries are respected, boundaries are sought out, and they are honored — and if they're not, then that is a problem. But, then, it's addressed. It's owned. It's corrected, amends are made, and you're okay at the end of it. I keep coming back because this is a place where I can feel safe emotionally, to say something I feel. I can actually express myself, I can risk saying something and know that if it doesn't land well, that we can talk through it. Or if I misinterpret something, I can ask questions and know I'm not going to be judged … You're given that leeway to actually be curious. And curiosity is something that drives me quite a bit.

curiosity is something that drives me

TATIANA

PRONOUNS	She/Her	RELATIONSHIP STATUS OR STRUCTURE	Polyamorous
GENDER IDENTITY	Queer Femme	AGE	33
SEXUAL ORIENTATION	Pansexual	LOCATION	Bay Area, California, U.S.

KINK IS THAT BUILDING OF TRUST WITH YOURSELF, AS WELL AS BUILDING THAT TRUST WITH OTHERS IN WAYS THAT, IN ORDER TO BE SAFE, FORCE YOU TO DIG DEEPER AND COMMUNICATE AND BE UNCOMFORTABLE. TO GET COMFORTABLE WITH BEING UNCOMFORTABLE, WHETHER THAT'S PHYSICALLY, MENTALLY, EMOTIONALLY.

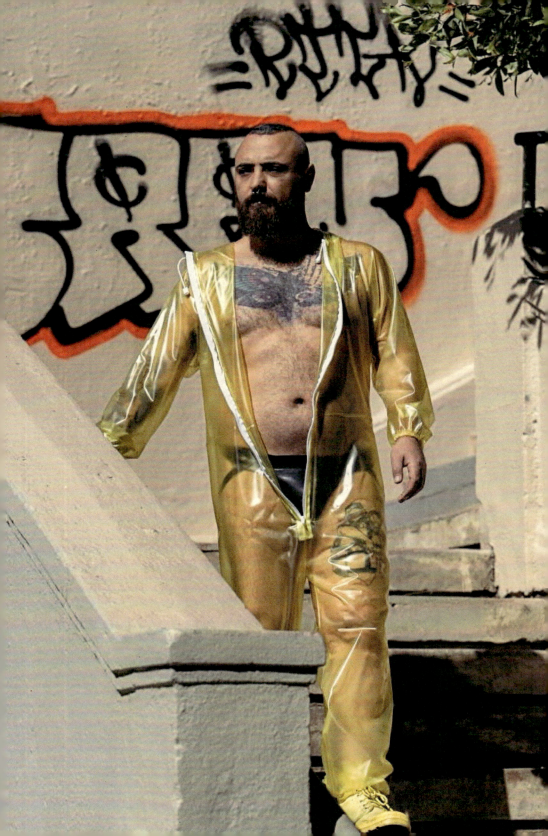

Kink can be visible sometimes and invisible other times, like all superpowers — and that's really how it feels for me. The thing that changes in me is how kink really helps me better understand myself, and better understand others. How I present in my body has been affected positively by kink. One of the most important things is the community that I was able to find. It instilled trust, and I feel supported. What I want in my mind and in my emotions, kink allows me to do.

x x x

With rope play, it doesn't need to be sexual. It could be erotic, but it doesn't need to lead to sex or even to orgasm. There is a really wide variety of experiences you can have with rope and bondage. Unless I'm gagging someone, I use verbal communication to check in throughout. With rope, like building a harness, or tying up wrists or hands, there are some techniques you can use, asking them to squeeze your hand when you grab it. And that will kind of tell you about their mobility. So there are these little things, and I tell them to keep an eye out on their nerves and to check in with me on what type of sensation they're feeling so there's no harm done. It's a continuous check-in all throughout the process, especially for new people. For example, my partner, my husband, I've been tying him up for five, six years now. I trained on him, so I know him well enough and he knows me well enough, that we don't need to speak as much. But we still maintain that communication because your body changes and you never know what you might be feeling during that particular scene.

JOHNNY

PRONOUNS	He/They	**RELATIONSHIP STATUS OR STRUCTURE**	Married
GENDER IDENTITY	███████	**AGE**	39
SEXUAL ORIENTATION	Gay	**LOCATION**	San Francisco, U.S.

KINK CAN BE VISIBLE SOMETIMES AND INVISIBLE OTHER TIMES, LIKE ALL SUPERPOWERS.

GUDRUN

PRONOUNS	██████	**RELATIONSHIP STATUS OR STRUCTURE**	██████
GENDER IDENTITY	Female	**AGE**	██████
SEXUAL ORIENTATION	Bisexual	**LOCATION**	Amsterdam, The Netherlands

BDSM gives me freedom and space in the head.

Normally in a relationship I easily have the upper hand due to my dominant nature, even though it's something I do not wish to happen. And when I do have this upper hand, I lose respect for my partner, and subsequently I lose interest in the erotic part.

When BDSM came into my life and I chose to be the submissive part with full power exchange, then I could finally let my guard down. I could finally relax in the head. This allowed me to let my sexual energy run freely and not be hindered by the stern voices in my head. It was still, it was calm, it was good.

After having had a long relationship that initially started out as a 24/7 power exchange, I learned that a 100% power exchange with micromanagement is something that is not feasible for me. Why? Because life on a daily basis catches up with you. During this relationship with full power exchange, I ran my own business, had employees, had a household with kids, and so to be in charge in those areas is a thing that comes natural and cannot just be overruled by an agreement to hand over power in these fields as well. So when that part of the agreement was broken, the rest crumbled down along with it and before we knew, I was back to having the upper hand in all fields. This broke up the relationship.

It has been a good experience, and I know now that I can't deny who I am, and that is someone who is almost always in charge. I then decided to be submissive only in the bedroom, and only by "play."

At the moment, I choose to be a toy for couples only: being sub for both or only the female part really attracts me. I like the idea of joining a couple for play, because they don't desire a relationship with me: they're already in a relationship together. And a relationship just doesn't fit into my life. Kink in the bedroom is enough, a play, a good time and then I sleep alone in my own be.

IT HAS BEEN A GOOD EXPERIENCE, AND I KNOW NOW THAT I CAN'T DENY WHO I AM, AND THAT IS **SOMEONE WHO IS ALMOST ALWAYS IN CHARGE.** I THEN DECIDED TO BE **SUBMISSIVE ONLY IN THE BEDROOM,** AND ONLY BY **"PLAY."**

My personal experience with kink is quite obviously genetic. Why else would I have come up with the idea to make a corset out of flooring supplies at the age of eight? That was also the first time that I realized I was different. My brother, who was four years older than me, caught me and ratted me out to our mother. She came into my room, pulled the comforter off of me, checked me out, covered me back up, and we never talked about the matter again. Ever.

My favorite kink is wearing corsets. I own 19 of them. I think they're really cool, both sexually and as a fashion statement. And there's a difference between me putting it on myself and someone else lacing me into it and telling me, "You're going to wear this for the next two hours!" Or for an event. That's more exciting and arousing than when I put it on myself.

x x x

If you have a successful kinky relationship and find the love of your life on top of that, it's really difficult when there's a rival who doesn't respect safe words. This was cancer in my wife Rosa's case. The letting go, the caretaking, was the ultimate experience of surrender. Losing her felt like open heart surgery without anesthesia. My doctor said that my heart attack was 50% genetics and 50% broken heart syndrome. But kink taught me to let go and to not suppress the feelings. Instead, I could fully embrace the process of grief and the dealing with the heart attack. And to let go of control. I don't think I would have been able to cope the way I did if I hadn't had experiences through kink.

TUA

PRONOUNS	He/She/It	**RELATIONSHIP STATUS OR STRUCTURE**	Widowed
GENDER IDENTITY	▇▇▇▇▇▇	**AGE**	71
SEXUAL ORIENTATION	Kink	**LOCATION**	Berlin, Germany

MY PERSONAL EXPERIENCE WITH KINK IS QUITE OBVIOUSLY GENETIC. WHY ELSE WOULD I HAVE COME UP WITH THE IDEA TO MAKE A CORSET OUT OF FLOORING SUPPLIES AT THE AGE OF EIGHT?

I don't go out as much as I used to, but sometimes when there's an event, I'll pull it together and I'll go and the kids are very happy to see me and they're encouraging me, saying they'd love for me to come to the play party. I jokingly look at them and say, *Darlin,' I'd rather kill you than play with you tomorrow night because I have only one or two events in my body per week*. And that's the best I can offer. I have to gauge what I can do and what I can't do at this age. Honey, you can't sustain it like you used to. But that doesn't mean you have to end everything. You just have to plan things.

x x x

In the end, just enjoy the lust and desire to play and the fun of all of it. If it's not fun, this isn't the place for you.

QUEEN COUGAR

PRONOUNS	She/Her	**RELATIONSHIP STATUS OR STRUCTURE**	Married
GENDER IDENTITY	Female	**AGE**	69
SEXUAL ORIENTATION	Leather Dyke Domme	**LOCATION**	San Francisco, U.S.

Racism is a part of the world that we live in. People come into the scene with everything they bring from their life and their experiences. So, there are going to be racists in the scene. That's part of life. You have to understand that as a person of color, and you have to govern yourself accordingly. That's something I talk about to kinksters, especially younger folks or those new to the scene: That it's perfectly fine to play with anybody you want to play with, matters not the color, matters not the nationality, none of that matters. What matters is the energy that you feel with that person. If you believe that person respects you and appreciates the gift that you are offering of yourself, then I don't care what anybody else has to say. But if you feel something is off, you have to acknowledge that. We have to learn to accept what we really feel because it's usually the truth.

x x x

I do have a strong blood fetish. I really enjoy playing with needles. I developed this fun thing of playing with several friends at some events where we do blow guns. It's a very traditional African activity that we have adapted to doing blowguns with needles into bodies. So exciting when the needle has hit a spot on someone, and the blood spurted out, and everyone went, *Oh, ooh, ah! It's like, Oh my God, we are so sick!* But it was also so wonderful. It's such incredible energy because blood is life.

x x x

I like to be a little wicked in the way that I play with people, and I giggle a little bit. Some people in the playrooms get really mad when we are laughing, some people are so intense and serious in their play, that they cannot stand laughter in the playroom, they don't think it's very "leather." Well, sometimes when you get to a certain level of endorphins, laughter is the only thing you're going to produce. But they don't think it's true kink, so I sometimes like to be wicked and force people to get to that point where they are laughing because they have experienced so much pain and they are so happy about it.

x x x

> it's perfectly fine to play with anybody you want to play with, matters not the color, matters not the nationality, none of that matters. What matters is the energy that you feel with that person. If you believe that person respects you and appreciates the gift that you are offering of yourself, then I don't care what anybody else has to say.

Here's the big secret about us kinksters: We're all just human beings. We have fears, we have personality issues, we have strengths and weaknesses. You never lose your humanity and the people that you're dealing with have to be seen as human beings, who have the possibility of being very, very good, or very, very dangerous. There are people who shadow themselves and come into the kink world with another agenda entirely, different than that of most of the people that I've spent my life playing with and enjoying time with. There are people who are very, very dangerous, and they do walk in our world. And we can't deny that. We have a problem with policing our community because we come into this wanting no clearing house, no gatekeepers. As a person of color, I have always been aware that anybody can be among us, and I have to stay aware.

Nowadays, it's become more the norm in all levels of experience in the community, to acknowledge people of color, and to openly welcome and encourage people of color to participate. When I first got involved in the scene, I realized that as a person of color, I'm basically stepping into a situation that's rife with possibility for people to abuse me. I made up my mind early on that I was never going to let that happen — no matter what I wanted to experience, no matter what I wanted to try, no matter who wanted to play with me. If I feel that at the root of it, they're doing it because they want to play with a Black woman and subjugate me in some way, and that's feeding some desire that comes from their experiences in life and who they are as a person, I would stop it immediately. And so that's how I pretty much govern myself. I feel people out.

THERE ARE PEOPLE WHO ARE VERY, VERY DANGEROUS, AND THEY DO WALK IN OUR WORLD. AND WE CAN'T DENY THAT. **WE HAVE A PROBLEM WITH POLICING OUR COMMUNITY** BECAUSE WE COME INTO THIS WANTING NO CLEARING HOUSE, NO GATEKEEPERS. AS A PERSON OF COLOR, I HAVE ALWAYS BEEN AWARE THAT ANYBODY CAN BE AMONG US, AND I HAVE TO STAY AWARE.

When I was about five or six, I had a large closet in my bedroom, and I took those little handcuffs that they would give you at the Dollar Store for a police costume, like for kids to play with, and proceeded to set up a little dungeon.

x x x

> my work on the femdom side of things has been largely to un-fuck those particular gender norms.

There is an extreme problem with female doms being pushed out of discovering their kinks due to a limited stereotype set of what you're allowed to be as a dominant. A significant number of women who might try it are simply unable to realize it due to a tendency, even within the BDSM community, for compulsory female submission as an assumption based on people's supposed gender roles. And my work on the femdom side of things has been largely to un-fuck those particular gender norms. A significant part of this work has been to combat the fact that there really isn't content created for dominant women. It's gotten better, but it is still largely all fetishization of doms; it's not fetishization for doms.

x x x

They say that a man who owns 100 high-heeled shoes is a fetishist and a pervert, and the woman who owns 100 high-heeled shoes is a collector and a fashionista. And I'm pretty damn sure that if she's talking about these being sexy shoes, she's just as much a fetishist as she is a collector.

MISS PEARL

PRONOUNS	She/Her or They/Them	RELATIONSHIP STATUS OR STRUCTURE	Married
GENDER IDENTITY	Woman or Non-Binary Woman	AGE	38
SEXUAL ORIENTATION	Gray Ace (gray asexual), bisexual as far as partner preference	LOCATION	Pacific Northwest, U.S.

THEY SAY THAT A MAN WHO OWNS 100 HIGH-HEELED SHOES IS A FETISHIST AND A PERVERT, AND THE WOMAN WHO OWNS 100 HIGH-HEELED SHOES IS A COLLECTOR AND A FASHIONISTA.

ZERO

PRONOUNS	He/Him	**RELATIONSHIP STATUS OR STRUCTURE**	Married, Polyamorous
GENDER IDENTITY	Male	**AGE**	61
SEXUAL ORIENTATION	Gay	**LOCATION**	San Francisco Bay Area, U.S.

> I'm supporting my Dom emotionally, just as much as he's supporting me, while I am being completely submissive to him. I don't think people get that.

I have a good friend who was talking to me about submission, and he asked me this question, which has stuck with me ever since. He said: "What's the difference between submission and just being lazy?" It's a really excellent question. Submission is not lazy sex, like, "Sure, you can decide what we do." It's not like that. It's actually giving up control. And, to me, that's what submission is about. I hesitate to say it's freeing, not because that sounds like a pretty common response, but because it implies that the rest of my life is not free. The freedom of submission lets me access a part of myself that I don't otherwise use, or am unable to get to. I can't get to that place if I'm in charge.

x x x

Something that we say a lot within the kink community — and I don't know that other people hear this — is that these things are consensual, negotiated power exchange. The guy isn't debasing himself to be a slave because he has, you know, no ego or no self-control. These experiences and these choices are our own. They are safe, sane, and consensual. The presented dynamic can appear very asymmetrical. But the support, love, and empowerment is completely symmetric. I'm supporting my Dom emotionally, just as much as he's supporting me, while I am being completely submissive to him. I don't think people get that. I'm not totally sure even I got that until I was in it for a while. But the love, the support, the empowerment, the humanization of each other, that's completely symmetric, even if everything you're watching, or experiencing, looks completely asymmetric and completely one-sided.

> But the love, the support, the empowerment, the humanization of each other, that's completely symmetric, even if everything you're watching, or experiencing, looks completely asymmetric and completely one-sided.

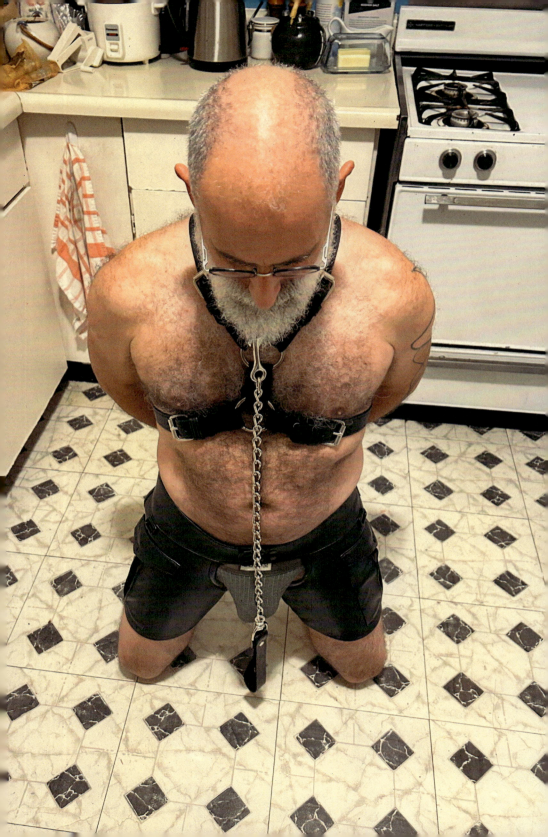

THE FREEDOM OF SUBMISSION LETS ME ACCESS A PART OF MYSELF THAT I DON'T OTHERWISE USE, OR AM UNABLE TO GET TO. I CAN'T GET TO THAT PLACE IF I'M IN CHARGE.

Being vanilla in and of itself is a kink. Doing missionary is a kink.

I think being vanilla is indeed a kink. I would say everybody is kinky whether they want to admit it or not. Some people just kind of have it repressed. I let it fly!

Kink, for me, is an escape. It's an escape from reality. I get to have this secret, to have this different persona, get into this different mindset for a while. For me, it's a way out. It's a way out from reality for me.

RAIN

PRONOUNS	She/He/They	RELATIONSHIP STATUS OR STRUCTURE	Single
GENDER IDENTITY	Trans Feminine	AGE	34
SEXUAL ORIENTATION	Gay	LOCATION	Oklahoma, U.S.

I THINK BEING VANILLA IS INDEED A KINK.

Once the hood goes on, once I'm in that headspace, it's so freeing and liberating. I'm no gender, just pup. No gender, just pony.

Everything that limits you, like your age, your gender, your race, your background, I think that all kind of just disappears and you're no longer one thing. Like the humanizing aspect of being a sub and also being a Dom. When you get into that headspace you're no longer a person, you're an animal, or you're a service animal, or you're a sex toy. You are just this thing. You are two bodies, two energies, two things working together, creating a scene and joy, creating some pleasure.

It's a weird and incredible thing that we are able to explore as people and as communities, as well. Kink and kinky love is so wholesome and welcome. And I just think it's very, very empowering.

SLUSH PUPPY

PRONOUNS	He/They/Slut/Pup	RELATIONSHIP STATUS OR STRUCTURE	Polyamorous
GENDER IDENTITY	Trans Masculine	AGE	25
SEXUAL ORIENTATION	Polysexual, Aromantic	LOCATION	Norfolk, U.K.

ONCE THE HOOD GOES ON, ONCE I'M IN THAT HEADSPACE, IT'S SO FREEING AND LIBERATING. I'M NO GENDER, JUST PUP. NO GENDER, JUST PONY.

EVERYTHING THAT LIMITS YOU, LIKE YOUR AGE, YOUR GENDER, YOUR RACE, YOUR BACKGROUND, I THINK THAT ALL KIND OF JUST DISAPPEARS AND YOU'RE NO LONGER ONE THING.

While I enjoy activities like impact play, edge play, knife play, fear play, I have a fondness for psychological play because I think the mind is the most incredible toy to play with. It's not a kink I practice with everyone because it requires getting to know someone in some depth. It is important to learn what parts of a person's psyche you can play with and what parts you need to leave alone. That takes time and trust to learn, so it's not something I usually do outside of relationships. You can't just go to a random dungeon party and ask someone: *Hey, will you let me destroy your mind tonight?*

x x x

> **Don't be lonely in the shadows. Find a community near you and be a part of something.**

Don't be lonely in the shadows. Find a community near you and be a part of something. You don't need to be silent. You don't need to hide. Of course, different parts of the world have different socio-economic situations and different cultural situations, but anywhere you live, there are going to be people like you, people who understand you, people who get you. Just be a part of a community and have a fuller life!

DIABLO

PRONOUNS	He/Him	**RELATIONSHIP STATUS OR STRUCTURE**	▮▮▮▮▮
GENDER IDENTITY	Man	**AGE**	48
SEXUAL ORIENTATION	Queer	**LOCATION**	San Francisco Bay Area, U.S.

I HAVE A FONDNESS FOR PSYCHOLOGICAL PLAY BECAUSE I THINK **THE MIND IS THE MOST INCREDIBLE TOY TO PLAY WITH.**

I WILL PUT A HEADSET ON THEM THAT MAY START OFF WITH LIGHT NOISE, OR RELAXATION MUSIC, THEN JUMP INTO BABIES CRYING FOR LONG PERIODS OF TIME. IT MAKES YOU WANT TO SCREAM. I MAY GO BACK DOWN TO SOOTHING MUSIC AND ALTERNATE. THEY'RE KEPT OFF GUARD.

Oh yes, I have Black friends. "So how many Black friends do you have?" She said, I have five Black friends. "So, do you count your white friends?" This is just an example of how I get into an interrogation.

SIR GUY

PRONOUNS	He/Him	**RELATIONSHIP STATUS OR STRUCTURE**	Master/slave Dynamic
GENDER IDENTITY	Cis Male	**AGE**	65
SEXUAL ORIENTATION	Heterosexual	**LOCATION**	South Carolina, U.S.

I'm into interrogation. I was a police officer and I also managed a security company for a while. I also worked for a collection agency helping people get Medicaid to pay hospital bills and I was an emergency medical technician for over 20 years. I had to be frank and ask personal questions. And I'm a very inquisitive person by nature. So being able to ask questions, and gain information is something that I do. Even in my volunteer work. I volunteered preparing people for job interviews, getting them prepared to answer certain questions that will likely be asked. All of those things come into where I find my kink. That cerebral part of kink, the interrogation part of it, it informs my outside interests.

> Sometimes you do what is called a "rendition," where a person is actually snatched up and they're taken from point A to point B. Sometimes their clothes are removed and they are given a shirt or a jumper with a number on it.

To create an interrogation scene, you have to set the scene and set the mood. I've been in it in different ways. Sometimes you do what is called a "rendition," where a person is actually snatched up and they're taken from point A to point B. Sometimes their clothes are removed and they are given a shirt or a jumper with a number on it. That dehumanizes the scene and depersonalizes it for both parties. You make sure that when they address you, when they answer you, they only answer to the number they've been given. I use blindfolds, I use some restraints. I will put a headset on them that may start off with light noise, or relaxation music, then jump into babies crying for long periods of time. It makes you want to scream. I may go back down to soothing music and alternate. They're kept off guard.

I do preparation before that. I check out their profile on something like FetLife. I read through their profile and see what type of groups they're in, what type of kinks that they have. I'll give you an example: I had one person who was part of a demo I was doing; I read her profile in which she said she was a proud, beer-swilling redneck.

So during the course of my interrogation, I said, "Oh you say you're a redneck?" She said yes. I said, "Oh, so you're proud of that. So you're a racist?" She said, no, I'm not a racist. I said, "Well, do you have Black friends?"

THAT CEREBRAL PART OF KINK, THE INTERROGATION PART OF IT, IT INFORMS MY OUTSIDE INTERESTS.

JIMJAM

PRONOUNS	He/Him	**RELATIONSHIP STATUS OR STRUCTURE**	Partnered
GENDER IDENTITY	Male	**AGE**	33
SEXUAL ORIENTATION	Pansexual	**LOCATION**	Dallas, Texas, U.S.

Kink pushes the boundaries of what's normal. It takes whatever society says is normal and asks, why is it that way? Why can't it be this way? It's something that you enjoy and something that takes you on a journey and it's something you love. Let's go into it. Why not? It's got a little bit of challenging of authority to it.

x x x

I love cigars. To me, this is an exchange of energy. I have put my energy and time into cultivating this ash. I have built this from my breath, from the time that I've spent, and now I am giving it to you. I am placing it on your body. I am placing it in your mouth. I am giving that energy and that effort to my bottom. I find it to be a very intimate connection. I also really like that it's a little bit messy, that it can be anywhere and everywhere. I remember at one social, I was going to give ash and it fell on my boot. My submissive was right there. I was like okay, well, it's on my boot — now clean my boot. I think that there's so much you can do with it. I have played with some burning. I haven't gotten too far with it. But I've seen it as well in multiple instances and ways. And I really love the ritual of the lighting of a cigar, having it cut, having it lit, having it presented. That ritual in itself is also a connection with that person of service.

x x x

I see a lot more kink in media. But I don't think that it is necessarily "correct" kink. I think that's where the problem lies, because kink itself is not portrayed in a way that is safe.

You have people coming in trying to do things like in *Fifty Shades of Grey* or *How to Build a Sex Room,* and not actually understand the fundamentals of the things to keep you safe, to understand the how and why behind everything.

KINK PUSHES THE BOUNDARIES OF WHAT'S NORMAL. IT TAKES WHATEVER SOCIETY SAYS IS NORMAL AND ASKS, *WHY IS IT THAT WAY? WHY CAN'T IT BE THIS WAY?* IT'S SOMETHING THAT YOU ENJOY AND **SOMETHING THAT TAKES YOU ON A JOURNEY AND IT'S SOMETHING YOU LOVE.** LET'S GO INTO IT. WHY NOT? IT'S GOT A LITTLE BIT OF CHALLENGING OF AUTHORITY TO IT.

> There's the creativity, the interaction, the beauty of the tools themselves. I like all those dimensions of the senses and how they get expanded through the kink interaction.

The area of kink that I love the most is rope and bondage. There's a beauty to the rope. There's a beauty to the human form and how you can push it to certain extremes. Suspension is a favorite. Doing extreme positions is a favorite. So I think it is a combination of yes, I'm pursuing sex, but there's something about pushing the boundaries of what the body can do. And also my own creativity. Where can my mind take me with a tool, in this case rope? I'm very organic in my approach. I just kind of respond to the moment and respond to how my submissive is responding to the interaction. There's the creativity, the interaction, the beauty of the tools themselves. I like all those dimensions of the senses and how they get expanded through the kink interaction.

SIR IVAN

PRONOUNS	He/Him	**RELATIONSHIP STATUS OR STRUCTURE**	Married, Polyamorous
GENDER IDENTITY	Male	**AGE**	61
SEXUAL ORIENTATION	Gay	**LOCATION**	Minneapolis, MN, U.S.

THERE'S A BEAUTY TO THE ROPE. THERE'S A BEAUTY TO THE HUMAN FORM AND HOW YOU CAN PUSH IT TO CERTAIN EXTREMES.

in the freezer. She had a blindfold on, and I fed her rose tea, ice cream, and fresh persimmons sliced very thin. I'm feeding her and she's moaning these soft purring moans.

I literally orgasmed from feeding her — *just exploded!* — from that connection. I didn't even know her that well, but we both cried afterward because it was so intimate. Neither of us had touched the other genitally. It was purely cerebral.

NUNCA

PRONOUNS	She/They	RELATIONSHIP STATUS OR STRUCTURE	Solo Polyamorous
GENDER IDENTITY	Salty Genderf@ck	AGE	53
SEXUAL ORIENTATION	Queer	LOCATION	Oakland, California, U.S.

> She was larger than life and when we touched for the first time, I melted into Her arms then dropped to my knees. It felt right and it felt real.

She was larger than life and when we touched for the first time, I melted into Her arms then dropped to my knees. It felt right and it felt real. But I was nervous because we hadn't negotiated anything, hadn't talked about sexual limits. I really wanted to get filthy, but what if she was more conservative when we got together in person? We had been playing online and on FaceTime for six months and now here we were, finally in the same physical space.

It was past midnight when we got back to my house. We were uncharacteristically quiet, and I had no idea how this was going to go. But I got my answer quickly. We parked, I took Her bags and lead Her inside my house in silence. She said She had to piss and asked where the bathroom was. When I told Her, she replied, "Take off your clothes and get in the shower. On your back." Delighted, I did as I was told and stretched out in the bathtub. She stepped in and positioned Herself above me, standing on the sides of the tub. Without uttering a word, she pulled down Her pants and drained Her full bladder onto my body, spraying every inch of me with Her warmth.

That was the first time I had such an exciting fantasy play out without planning and without words. The silence and the mystery added to the eroticism of the scene. Based on trust and instinct, it was a true energy exchange, and it was raw as fuck. It was pure magic. Kink, Leather magic.

x x x

I once had a scene with a woman who orgasmed without me ever touching her genitals. I was spanking, cropping, and flogging her. The most amazing part of the whole thing was after she came, I was feeling a little bit like I was being a service top. I thought: *That was cool for her, but what about me, you know?*

I didn't quite know what to do with her or myself at that point, because we hadn't negotiated intimacy. And I don't know what made me think of it, but I had fresh persimmons off my mother's tree, and I had really good vanilla ice cream

In my personal and professional life, I am a dog trainer and a devoted dog rescue volunteer. What drew me to this lifestyle is the same thing that drew me to kink and leather: structure, protocol, intensity, and the whole-hearted devotion to a lifestyle that incorporates all of these elements. Canine brains and neurodivergent brains both need healthy structure to thrive. I will push myself in positive ways if I have structure. But if I don't have a mapped-out schedule, positive reinforcement, regular exercise, meal plans, relationships built on trust and open communication, I can spiral into some pretty dark places. But when I'm healthy I can dive into dark places that are actually a fun place to exist. Places where kink and leather take me.

I think I also got into dogs because I had a lot of trouble maintaining human relations. I didn't understand how to get my needs met or to develop healthy intimacy with people. The use of body language, patience, and other nonverbal communication with dogs and the newfound use of words and conversation with kink negotiation, I have been able to find a deeper understanding of myself.

It's no surprise that I have found my closest and most rewarding relationships through kink and leather. My leather siblings are my chosen family. The core of the leather lifestyle is trust, integrity, respect, communication, growth, learning, negotiation, consent, STRUCTURE. It makes me feel safe, so I am free to be my authentic self, and that spreads into every area of my life. It has even improved communication with my parents, which was never very good, and is now better than ever. But most importantly, I have achieved clarity and respect for my own boundaries and can successfully negotiate my own needs and my needs within relationships.

x x x

I identify as a raunch pig, so I've done quite a bit of what goes beyond a lot of people's limits. Because I'm also into consent, I usually have a lot of negotiation and keep a slow pace when getting involved with people. I did have one relationship that got so hot so fast that it took me by surprise. I'm not normally the "s" in the Dominant/submissive dynamic. But I had met this new person online and we hit it off so much that we just clicked into this dynamic of Sir/boi. I flew Her out from the East Coast so we could finally meet in person and find out if this thing was real. When I picked Her up from the airport it was magical.

I FED HER ROSE TEA, ICE CREAM, AND FRESH PERSIMMONS SLICED VERY THIN. I'M FEEDING HER AND SHE'S MOANING THESE SOFT PURRING MOANS.

Now, years later, I teach classes called "Kindness and Other Kinks." And we talk about that particular scene and everybody in the class gets a notebook. Inside, it says:

This started as a thank you gift for people who played with me and it eventually became my trademark. They're given out to people I have developed a connection with in life, whether a chance meeting or a longtime relationship. When I give you a notebook, it shows that I care about you. The purpose of this book is to take inventory of your small victories, compliments, good things, and what brings you joy. When you're having a bad day, I want you to go back and read it to yourself and remember the positive difference you are making in others' lives just by being who you are. Be well and always be good to yourself.

I've given out nearly 300 notebooks both in kink workshops and in my profession, because I teach new employees at a major bank. Nobody they ever worked for had reminded them to be good to themselves. I ended up winning an award for that at work. But it is the epitome of what I feel about the kink community. It gives us the opportunity to remember why we need to be kind to ourselves, even though some of us may want to feel the hurt in order to be kind.

HITHERECATSUIT

PRONOUNS	He/Him/They/Them	RELATIONSHIP STATUS OR STRUCTURE	▮▮▮▮▮
GENDER IDENTITY	Genderfluid	AGE	61
SEXUAL ORIENTATION	Straight	LOCATION	Cincinnati, Ohio, U.S

She wanted me to see me

The whole scene culminated with me on my knees looking into her eyes, and she said: "If my eyes leave you, you will feel the most abandoned that you ever have. So do not leave the space in my eyes." And I'm there practically shaking and she asks, "What do you see?" And I said, "I see beauty." She responded, "Well, that's good because it's only a reflection." And I started sobbing so hard that it was hard for me to recover. She wanted me to see me for who other people see. I actually teach classes now in the things that she taught me in that scene. I teach classes on kindness of how people can see themselves in different ways. That one scene affected me more than any other scene and it had not one bit of restraint. Not one bit of impact. Not one bit of pain. But it was the most emotional scene I ever had.

x x x

I met up with a friend of mine at a kink gathering. She'd gained 80 pounds after a bad breakup and hadn't been to an event in a long time. She didn't feel she belonged. I decided to stay around while she did a scene. She's tied with both arms at her side and blindfolded, and she's receiving impact. Pretty hard impact, too, because she's very much a masochist. In between the impacts, I went up and whispered in her ear, "You realize how beautiful you are right now?" And then, quietly, I gathered all her friends and each of them went up and said something to her. At the end of the scene, they took her hands down and they took her blindfold off and all her friends were gathered in front of her. I was standing there, holding a notebook, and in it we had written all the things we had said to her. "The purpose of this notebook is to remind you that you did belong here. And you do belong here. And when you're having a crappy day, go back and read it."

IT GIVES US THE OPPORTUNITY TO REMEMBER WHY **WE NEED TO BE KIND TO OURSELVES,** EVEN THOUGH SOME OF US MAY WANT TO FEEL THE HURT IN ORDER TO BE KIND.

I define kink as someone who puts in extra energy toward their sexual fulfillment.

A kinkster's ability is to lay out our boundaries, but also to put our trust in another person doing what they say they're going to do. Kink creates this nice dynamic and energy that goes on between the people at play, and then almost creates a third energy. It's kind of a third element, not something we can physically see. It's within that third space that you can really explore and have a kink experience with freedom and vulnerability, and then express and heal within it.

x x x

I think the biggest thing that I would like to convey to everyone is just how absolutely normal being in the kink community is. It's really no different than a bowling league.

BUFFY LEE

PRONOUNS	She/Her	RELATIONSHIP STATUS OR STRUCTURE	Ethically Non-Monogamous
GENDER IDENTITY	Female	AGE	49
SEXUAL ORIENTATION	Bisexual	LOCATION	Southern California, U.S.

I THINK THE BIGGEST THING THAT I WOULD LIKE TO CONVEY TO EVERYONE IS JUST HOW **ABSOLUTELY NORMAL** BEING IN THE KINK COMMUNITY IS. **IT'S REALLY NO DIFFERENT THAN A BOWLING LEAGUE.**

FLICKER

PRONOUNS	She/He	**RELATIONSHIP STATUS OR STRUCTURE**	in a platonic, vanilla relationship with my primary partner, plus boy and lover to my Sir
GENDER IDENTITY	Genderfluid Butch	**AGE**	54
SEXUAL ORIENTATION	Queer	**LOCATION**	▓▓▓▓▓▓▓▓

Kink definitely intersects with a lot of the other parts of my life, from the secular to the sacred.

On the secular side, it has made me more aware of how to project power, and how to refrain from projecting power. I can come across as somewhat intimidating to people, as a professor. I don't want to add any more intimidation, since my students are already going to be somewhat intimidated by me. I don't want to add to that anxiety. I'm not willing to make myself small for them, but I can make myself approachable, and easy to be with. In other situations, I might want to project a little more dominance, because that's going to be useful. And I'm much more aware of how to be intentional about that because of kink.

On the sacred side, I'm a Quaker, and Quakerism intersects with everything. But it's in my spiritual life and as a Quaker that my kink and life intersect. There are so many ways that BDSM can really strip us down, and create space for transformation and love. What I see happening in the dungeon, when people do a certain thing, is a chance for parts of us to be seen and loved and witnessed that we don't normally get an opportunity to share.

People store emotions and feelings in their bodies. People store grief in their bodies, people store fear and anxiety and anger in their bodies. I find as a top that I'm sometimes able, through touch, through pain, to release these feelings of grief, anger, anxiety, fear. It's not a permanent transformation, but sometimes it gives people the space they need to feel something different. And that feels like ministry to me. All of it feels like an opening for divine love to enter the world.

There's a popular perception that kink is sex, and it's just sex. It can be, if that's what you want it to be. But it can also be a place where people can explore other possibilities for themselves. Kink can be about love. It can be about mutual vulnerability. It can be where people can put something down for a while. I have seen people try out new genders in kink. That is where they first start exploring living as someone else. I have seen people taste what it is to be weak and vulnerable, when that isn't something that is safe for them to do in their regular lives. And I see all of these as openings for love to move through the world.

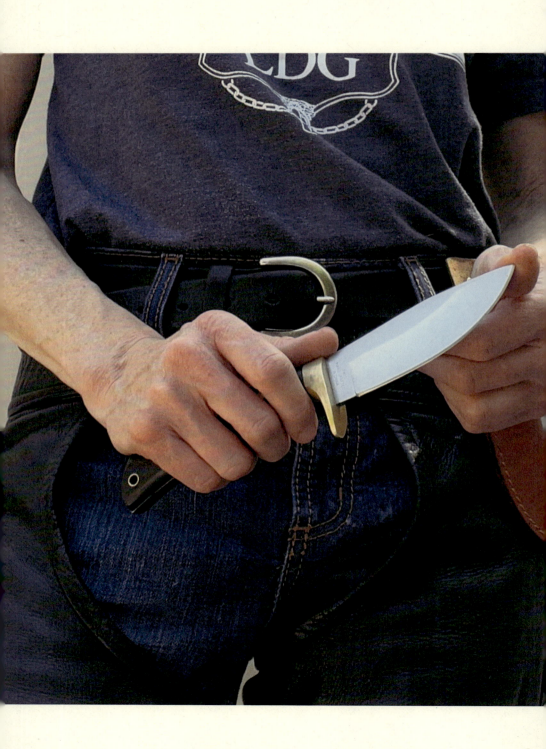

KINK DEFINITELY INTERSECTS WITH A LOT OF THE OTHER PARTS OF MY LIFE, FROM THE **SECULAR** TO THE **SACRED.**

I think the most important thing to share with non-kinksters about us is that we're doing this with love, with benevolence, with kindness, and with compassion. Even those of us who do really, really heavily sadomasochistic scenes. I'm a sadist. I love blood play. I love hurting consensual people. That's the thing I enjoy. Key concept here is: People who consent. I have an incredible amount of love and respect and admiration for my bottoms and for myself. These are real relationships … They may only last two or three or four hours, plus a couple of exchanges by email. I have people I've known for many years who I've been playing with, and they occupy a very, very special place in my heart. Yes, what we do can look extreme from the outside. But for us, it's not. It's all a matter of perspective … I think that it's essential to understand that what we're doing is relative to our needs, and also to the knowledge that most of us have. We do this with attention and with the intention of doing good to the other person, even if doing good means physically or emotionally hurting them consensually. And I think it can be really, really difficult to understand that from a more "vanilla" perspective. Sometimes, even I see things that I don't understand, like where a form of humiliation or some sort of pain could be pleasurable. But it's not up to me to judge what he or she or they think is pleasurable. That's up to them to define that with their partner.

INANNA JUSTICE

PRONOUNS	She/Her	**RELATIONSHIP STATUS OR STRUCTURE**	
GENDER IDENTITY		**AGE**	
SEXUAL ORIENTATION		**LOCATION**	Paris, France

> And I've just got a hunger for knowledge, which is wonderful in this community because it's endless. I'm always learning ...

I'm one of the only pro dommes that I know of who actually has to thank *Fifty Shades of Grey*. Even though the book was really problematic, it was thanks to that book that I discovered the vocabulary of BDSM. That was 12 years ago. BDSM, power exchange, kinkiness has been a part of my sexuality since my early days. I just didn't have the words around it until that book. At that point, I became really involved in the BDSM community, started attending munches, started getting play partners who were specifically for kink activities. And I've just got a hunger for knowledge, which is wonderful in this community because it's endless. I'm always learning ... and it's really wonderful to be constantly pushed to learn more, to keep developing my hard skills, the physical skills, whether that's flogging or whipping, or the psychological skills, which in D/s relationships, dominant-submissive relationships, is so important.

x x x

I love penetration play, you know, getting back to that idea of being very tactile. I love occupying the same space as my partner, whether that's anal or vaginal penetration, putting fingers in someone's mouth. Sounding is also a practice that I love.

x x x

I think that it's becoming more and more acceptable and comfortable for women to seek out pleasure with professionals. We have the right to sexuality, we have the right to pleasure how we want it, when we want it, and with whom we want. And so that's really promising for me. I'd like to see more and more women seeing professionals, whether that's professional escorts — escort boys, escort women, dominatrixes, pro subs. Historically, of course, it wasn't financially accessible for a lot of women and that's starting to change, thankfully.

x x x

WE'RE DOING THIS WITH LOVE, WITH BENEVOLENCE, WITH KINDNESS, AND WITH COMPASSION.

Kink has taught me to accept others as they are, not as I want them to be. That really is what everything boils down to in the kink community: not yucking someone else's yum. It's a hard skill for some people to learn, which is to accept others' kinks, even if they don't personally appeal to you.

One of my friends has been an advocate of scat play for many years and we've had this conversation many times.

He'll say something like, "So you're not gonna, you know, put me down because I like scat play?"

And I'll say, "No, no, no. It's not my thing. But you know, what? Tell me more about how much you're enjoying it, because I want to know *why* you enjoy it."

He'll say, "Ooh, you *are* kinky!"

And I'll reply, "I'm just accepting."

So acceptance of people *as they are,* I think, is the biggest thing kink has brought me.

MR. ALLAN

PRONOUNS	He/Him	**RELATIONSHIP STATUS OR STRUCTURE**	Polyamorous/Polycule
GENDER IDENTITY	Male	**AGE**	63
SEXUAL ORIENTATION	Gay	**LOCATION**	California, U.S.

KINK HAS TAUGHT ME TO **ACCEPT OTHERS AS THEY ARE,** NOT AS I WANT THEM TO BE. THAT REALLY IS WHAT EVERYTHING BOILS DOWN TO IN THE KINK COMMUNITY: **NOT YUCKING SOMEONE ELSE'S YUM.**

SO ACCEPTANCE OF PEOPLE AS THEY ARE, I THINK, IS THE BIGGEST THING KINK HAS BROUGHT ME.

het people and queer people and trans people and gay people and bi people all together as one community. Oh, do I miss that. Now when the community gets bigger, it tends to fragment and everybody goes off and plays in their own space, and that doesn't feel like home to me.

x x x

A lot of kink today seems too performative to me. Little about it feels like love, like connection. That's not what I got into kink for. If nobody is opening themselves up, then I'm not interested. I see a lot of tops who seem to be tops or Doms because it means they don't have to be vulnerable. And such a person is never going to lay their hand on my pretty pink hide, ever.

x x x

> every now and again I see something that just makes my jaw drop, and I love that.

I've been doing kink for 30 years and it's easy to get a little blasé when you've been doing this as long as I have. And yet, every now and again I see something that just makes my jaw drop, and I love that. I love that people are so incredibly diverse and innovative. That I with all my time ingrained in this community I can still get blown out of my chair by it. That's a source of great joy to me.

JANET W. HARDY

PRONOUNS	She/Her	**RELATIONSHIP STATUS OR STRUCTURE**	Married, in an open relationship
GENDER IDENTITY	Non-Binary	**AGE**	70
SEXUAL ORIENTATION	Bisexual Switch	**LOCATION**	Eugene, Oregon, U.S.

of bliss puddle. And nothing about this scene was what I would tell people to do in a first scene with a new person, particularly an inexperienced new person. But we both still remember it with tremendous fondness.

x x x

I would like people to understand why we do what we do, what we get from kink, besides all the neurochemical stuff that happens when we play close to our personal edges, whether those are emotional or physical, or sexual or whatever.

I like to use theater as a metaphor. Most people understand why we go to the theater and see things that are stressful or depressing or frightening. It's because we learn from it and we react to it emotionally. And I think that's still probably the metaphor I like best for what we do.

Kink is about altered states of consciousness and how we get there. It is a conceptually symbolic enactment of things that would not be okay, if it were not both consensual and symbolic. It's a symbolism that we as humans react to in a non-symbolic way.

Kink is consensual, mindful codependence, where you are consciously moving into the other person's emotional space and sharing it in a way that would be unhealthy if you did it outside the firewall that we put around our kink. All the safe words, all the safety training, all the workshops and conferences and things that we learn at those, are always how we make it safe to play with something that would be unsafe otherwise.

x x x

With the mainstreaming of kink, I like that nobody will have to go through what I did. There were years of my life when I honestly believed I was the only person in the world who got turned on thinking about spanking because I had no access to information to the contrary. So, nobody has to feel alone or shamed by their kink desires anymore.

x x x

This was true back when I was new. And I still see this in some small towns, and I love it. When the kink community is so small that it's all there is, and you get

I have both given and received uncountable spankings. I've enjoyed nearly all of them. And even the ones I didn't enjoy a lot, still felt okay. But at their best, what I want is an altered state of consciousness and a profound connection.

x x x

I don't choose my kink partners based on their sex or their gender. More on their presence, their willingness to be present, their willingness to be vulnerable, and that doesn't matter whether I'm talking top or bottom. I'm pretty indiscriminate. Ask anyone.

> what I want is an altered state of consciousness and a profound connection.

x x x

I'm pretty much a safeword absolutist. I've played on two occasions with bottoms who want to do a no-safeword scene, but the closest I was willing to come was to tell them that they could not safeword because the scene was too intense — that's what they were asking for. They were required, however, to safeword if they felt ill, or at physical or emotional risk, or for any other reason besides "this hurts too much."

Safewords exist for the top's protection as well as the bottom's. I've negotiated with one or two people who insist that they "can't" safeword. Color me dubious — but either way, I won't play under those circumstances, because I can't read minds and it's asking me to run a risk of harming someone without meaning to.

A friend of a friend, who'd never played in public before, really, really wanted me to spank her. So, this woman shows up and she's lovely. I started spanking her and it just went zero to 60. I'm not sure why, what it was I was getting from her that made that okay, but I beat the holy living crap out of her. We both went into a really ecstatic space with it and wound up at the climax just seizing each other and crumbling to the floor in this sort

> I don't choose my kink partners based on their sex or their gender. More on their presence, their willingness to be present, their willingness to be vulnerable, and that doesn't matter whether I'm talking top or bottom. I'm pretty indiscriminate. Ask anyone.

KINK IS ABOUT ALTERED STATES OF CONSCIOUSNESS AND HOW WE GET THERE. IT IS **A CONCEPTUALLY SYMBOLIC ENACTMENT OF THINGS THAT WOULD NOT BE OKAY, IF IT WERE NOT BOTH CONSENSUAL AND SYMBOLIC.** IT'S A SYMBOLISM THAT WE AS HUMANS REACT TO IN A NON-SYMBOLIC WAY.

AYZAD

PRONOUNS	He/Him	**RELATIONSHIP STATUS OR STRUCTURE**	Polyamorous
GENDER IDENTITY	Male	**AGE**	55
SEXUAL ORIENTATION	Heterosexual	**LOCATION**	Italy

> I once found myself in the hands of this wonderful, experienced woman and what I felt was not arousal or fear or pleasure or whatever, but "satori," the connection with the universe.

The focus in kink for me is not a specific scenario or practice but finding that one thing that moves the other person the most, that somehow opens some inner door or creates a deeper connection, a deeper understanding. And it may be something as simple as finding the right word, or as complex as creating an almost mad-scientist scenario. The big emotion, the big excitement for me, and the biggest actual arousal comes from that, from being able to shuttle people from one stage to another.

My early explorations were as a sub, and I once found myself in the hands of this wonderful, experienced woman and what I felt was not arousal or fear or pleasure or whatever, but "satori," the connection with the universe. I actually remember, after so many years, this sensation of total connection with the universe. And in the end this other person said: "Did I hurt you so badly, because you were crying so much?" They were tears of joy, of not having the burden of having to appear as something different than what I am, or hiding some part of me. And actually feeling the person as she really was, not as a mask, as a role. That was incredibly emotional. I think that human connection in general is great when it can make you feel like that. And maybe kink is not the only way. Surely it isn't. But it beats recusing yourself in a cave for 30 years and meditating. You even get to have orgasms. So, *Yay kink!*

> They were tears of joy, of not having the burden of having to appear as something different than what I am, or hiding some part of me.

THE FOCUS IN KINK FOR ME IS NOT A SPECIFIC SCENARIO OR PRACTICE BUT FINDING THAT ONE THING THAT MOVES THE OTHER PERSON THE MOST, THAT SOMEHOW OPENS SOME INNER DOOR OR CREATES A DEEPER CONNECTION, A DEEPER UNDERSTANDING.

FENNEC FORTUNE

PRONOUNS	She/They	**RELATIONSHIP STATUS OR STRUCTURE**	Polyamorous
GENDER IDENTITY	Trans Woman	**AGE**	▮▮▮
SEXUAL ORIENTATION	Pansexual	**LOCATION**	Bay Area, California, U.S.

> And impact play is such an unusually wonderful experience because you're consensually accepting smacks, hits, whips, sometimes a bit of pain. But that pain turns into serotonin and into adrenaline. And with the act of consent, you can say no whenever you want. It feels quite empowering.

Before I discovered the kink community, I definitely considered myself a pushover. I didn't really talk a lot. I always felt like I needed to apologize for existing. I was very, very meek. And now, being accepted for who I am, brought up so much confidence in myself. I sit up with a better posture, I am able to communicate better. Not just hearing my voice but also giving safe space for other people who are in a position where they feel they can't talk or they're feeling they're getting overshadowed by other people. I try to make sure that everything's consensual, that everything's equal. I stand up for myself, I stand up for others. I am now taking the space that I need and showing others that they can do the same. I believe in myself now to a point where I am taking on a project that I thought was impossible for myself, which is going back to school. And so I'm actually going to become a massage therapist.

I was terrified of physical touch before. I could give friends hugs, but no longer than a couple of seconds. Understanding how I interact with people through physical touch, I find super healing. Even just having a longer hug of five seconds. And impact play is such an unusually wonderful experience because you're consensually accepting smacks, hits, whips, sometimes a bit of pain. But that pain turns into serotonin and into adrenaline. And with the act of consent, you can say no whenever you want. It feels quite empowering.

I have to say that when I was younger, I got beat up a lot, hit a lot, and stuff like that. So having the power to be like, *Okay, I want to get hit, I want to get smacked,* brings a level of healing and joy that I never felt I could experience, to be honest.

BEFORE I DISCOVERED THE KINK COMMUNITY, I DEFINITELY CONSIDERED MYSELF A PUSHOVER. I DIDN'T REALLY TALK A LOT. I ALWAYS FELT LIKE I NEEDED TO APOLOGIZE FOR EXISTING. I WAS VERY, VERY MEEK. AND NOW, BEING ACCEPTED FOR WHO I AM, BROUGHT UP SO MUCH CONFIDENCE IN MYSELF. I SIT UP WITH A BETTER POSTURE, I AM ABLE TO COMMUNICATE BETTER.

To non-kinksters, I say this: "Stop believing the porn version."

x x x

Pieces of our identity develop partly because kink is innate, I guess, and partly because of what we're exposed to. I think I discovered my interest in kink much later in life, because I didn't run into it before. I think it's probably a good thing that it was later in life. When I started this, exploring kink, I was at a point in my life where I really, really didn't give a fuck what anybody else thought about it. I was not threatened by it. I didn't have to worry about losing my job. I didn't worry about my family. I didn't worry about my friends. And I didn't feel the need to be appalled by it, to justify, to rationalize, or anything—and that would not have been the case 10 years earlier. That would have been hard.

What do you discover when you discover what you're like?

LYLE SWALLOW

PRONOUNS	He/Him	**RELATIONSHIP STATUS OR STRUCTURE**	Polyamorous, in an Master/slave relationship serving a Master
GENDER IDENTITY	Male	**AGE**	72
SEXUAL ORIENTATION	Gay	**LOCATION**	San Francisco, U.S.

WHAT DO YOU DISCOVER WHEN YOU DISCOVER WHAT YOU'RE LIKE?

My very favorite kink, which is what I teach about, is pegging. It started off as a very gendered word that was all about a woman putting on a strap-on and penetrating a man anally. The gender binary is evolving and breaking down, so I now define pegging as anybody putting on a strap-on and penetrating someone who has a prostate or used to have a prostate, because sometimes they get removed.

x x x

The requirement for a healthy BDSM relationship is a negotiated, consensual, Dominant / submissive dynamic. It requires so much conversation and communication and negotiation that I'm just blown away when I dip my toes into the "vanilla" world. The vanillas don't know what they're doing. They don't know how to communicate. I know that's a generalization, but at the same time — oh! do the kinksters have it down with the whole communication and negotiation thing.

RUBY RYDER

PRONOUNS	She/Her	**RELATIONSHIP STATUS OR STRUCTURE**	Ethically Non-Monogamous
GENDER IDENTITY	Female	**AGE**	66
SEXUAL ORIENTATION	Straight	**LOCATION**	Southern California, U.S.

IT REQUIRES SO MUCH CONVERSATION AND COMMUNICATION AND NEGOTIATION THAT I'M JUST BLOWN AWAY WHEN I DIP MY TOES INTO THE "VANILLA" WORLD. THE VANILLAS DON'T KNOW WHAT THEY'RE DOING. THEY DON'T KNOW HOW TO COMMUNICATE. I KNOW THAT'S A GENERALIZATION, BUT AT THE SAME TIME — OH! DO THE KINKSTERS HAVE IT DOWN WITH THE WHOLE COMMUNICATION AND NEGOTIATION THING.

> There's a childlike self-exploration, that is really about getting to return to and experience your own body in a thrilling way.

Kink has brought me to an absolutely authentic and fearless place. I have no shame, I have no apologies for who I am, for what I like, for the strength and bravery that kink requires. It has utterly changed how I communicate, how I express my needs, my boundaries. It has improved me, in how I connect really deeply in listening to somebody else to hear their needs and boundaries more fully. For me, it has been a freeing shift of mind about how we build trust with another person.

PAPA

PRONOUNS	He/Him	RELATIONSHIP STATUS OR STRUCTURE	Married/Polyamorous
GENDER IDENTITY	Male	AGE	57
SEXUAL ORIENTATION	Gay	LOCATION	Southeastern U.S.

I did not come to kink until I was middle-aged. I had gone through a really, really traumatic and terrible surgery and it was devastating in terms of pain and what eventually became body dysmorphia for me. I felt my body had been ruined. I felt completely detached and disempowered from my own physical self.

> **It felt like glorious revenge, like a triumph!**

I found my kink journey with some guidance of loving people who saw what I was going through. It became part of healing and loving my body in all kinds of new, thrilling, and mildly frightening ways. It let me feel in control of my physical self again, including the pain that had redefined my body. Kink felt hyper-connective in terms of communication, vulnerability, honesty. It allowed me to find a route between pain and pleasure. It literally was like a somatic reprogramming for me: What had been so traumatizing could now be very empowering. It felt like glorious revenge, like a triumph!

I had a pretty heteronormative idea of sex prior to the transformative power of kink in my life. When you are disabled, as I am, or have unresolved trauma, kink can help you literally re-member your body and put the pieces of it back together in a way that authentically works. Being in control of pain is mind blowing. What hurt so badly gets transformed from a violence to something mastered within the self.

Kink, for me, is freedom. It's safety to explore. It's an indulgence or an experiment of an idea that has captured my mind. It is both very cerebral and very animalistic for me. I think once you recognize that sex and sexuality and gender are all constructs, and you can put them together however you want, then kink gives you permission to recombine all these fundamentals in a way that works for your life and body at the time. There's a childlike self-exploration, that is really about getting to return to and experience your own body in a thrilling way.

KINK HAS BROUGHT ME TO AN ABSOLUTELY AUTHENTIC AND FEARLESS PLACE. I HAVE NO SHAME, I HAVE NO APOLOGIES FOR WHO I AM, FOR WHAT I LIKE, FOR THE STRENGTH AND BRAVERY THAT KINK REQUIRES.

I work in marketing for a machine shop. And it is a cisgender, male-dominated world where a female voice either scares them, or they dismiss it. So my "top voice," I guess you could say, has actually helped with the customer service. It's more authoritative, and no one questions it. It's kind of fun.

x x x

What keeps me coming back for more is the safety of kink. It's not the cutting or the bondage or the asphyxiation, the risk, the edge of it. For me, it is the safety of it. It's totally not like what you would find in a movie or a book or something like that. It's the safety of the intimacy.

COCO

PRONOUNS	She/Her	**RELATIONSHIP STATUS OR STRUCTURE**	Married
GENDER IDENTITY	▮▮▮▮	**AGE**	▮▮
SEXUAL ORIENTATION	▮▮▮▮	**LOCATION**	San Francisco, U.S.

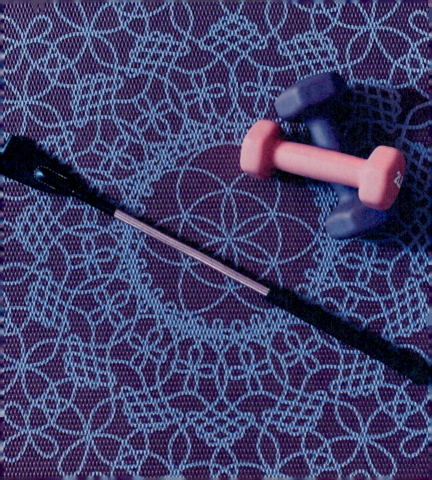

WHAT KEEPS ME COMING BACK FOR MORE IS **THE SAFETY OF KINK**. IT'S NOT THE CUTTING OR THE BONDAGE OR THE ASPHYXIATION, THE RISK, THE EDGE OF IT. FOR ME, IT IS THE SAFETY OF IT. **IT'S TOTALLY NOT LIKE WHAT YOU WOULD FIND IN A MOVIE OR A BOOK** OR SOMETHING LIKE THAT. **IT'S THE SAFETY OF THE INTIMACY.**

> Even if you don't understand, just accept that what works for me isn't necessarily going to work for everybody, but it certainly works for me.

The thing I'd like people to know about kink and the kinkster community is that there is so much joy and love and support. I think people see the outward side of it, with the leather and the impact play, or the denial or the humiliation or the piss play — things that seem to be degradation. There is so much freedom within that and so much catharsis from it. It makes me want to cry. One of the things that my Sir told me years ago was: "You don't know how strong you are. You are such a strong individual." And when I feel weak, that helps me feel strong. Knowing I have been bruised to the point where I can't sit down, and that's okay. I feel better and stronger knowing I can handle that. As a society, especially Americans, we can be so puritanical and frightened of the unknown. Even if you don't understand, just accept that what works for me isn't necessarily going to work for everybody, but it certainly works for me.

MIKEY

PRONOUNS	He/Him	**RELATIONSHIP STATUS OR STRUCTURE**	Single
GENDER IDENTITY	Male	**AGE**	50
SEXUAL ORIENTATION	Gay	**LOCATION**	Cincinnati, Ohio, U.S.

THE THING I'D LIKE PEOPLE TO KNOW ABOUT KINK AND THE **KINKSTER COMMUNITY** IS THAT THERE IS SO MUCH **JOY** AND **LOVE** AND SUPPORT.

What I love about our situation is that kink has become integrated into our normal lives. I'm a huge nerd. So we have monthly board game parties, and our friends come over. I try to keep it to the kinky homo crowd, because that's where we feel most comfortable. But my slave's always naked. I yell out things or orders, because I'm selfish and I want drinks at times. Our dynamic is normal for us, and because of the friends that we have integrated into our lives, they have come to expect us to just be that way. So they're okay with having a naked person going around and me yelling out random orders. And they respect it. It's not disturbing to them, which makes us feel that much more comfortable in our own life. We feel stable. We feel like we are progressing in life. So it's not something that we need to hide. That's what I want to be able to show to the world, in a sense, that you can have these alternative lifestyles that still work with the rest of the world. We're not pushing our lives on other couples or families that live next to us. We're not forcing our neighbors to follow our personal protocols, because that would just be weird. We just live our lives.

TYGER YOSHI | TYGER'S SLAVE

PRONOUNS	He/Him	**RELATIONSHIP STATUS OR STRUCTURE**	Consensual Owner/slave Partnership
GENDER IDENTITY	Male	**AGE**	40	52
SEXUAL ORIENTATION	Gay	**LOCATION**	Denver, Colorado, U.S.

Tyger:
My understanding of kink would be anything considered out of the "norm," which is extremely vague. How do you truly define what is normal, what is standard? For me, kink is actually my normal. It's weird when people ask, "What is your kink?" To me, my kink is my vanilla.

For me and my slave, we do have this power dynamic. I am a sadist. So I enjoy inflicting pain and watching my partners, as long as they're consenting, to have that struggle in them. Bondage is a huge part of my identity as well. It's become our lifestyle in a sense. So, kink is kind of like our normal.

Slave:
I'm at a point where I don't really have a border anymore. Kink is normal. For me, kink would almost be vanilla sex.

I once had a master who was a switch. It was great for me to be able to get the experience of being in the driving position. It was fun because he would order me to top him, and even when he was fully restrained, fully vulnerable, he was still ordering me to do things to him. That worked really well because I enjoyed hurting him when he wanted me to hurt him. That was a great dynamic.

Tyger:
The one thing that I want non-kinky people to know about kinksters is that like every other community out there, every other niche community, we have a spectrum of people who will have their own opinions and values. Our community just happens to be connected through this common interest of exploring our sexual natures beyond the vanilla. We are more willing and open to be more intimate with our bodies, with our own selves, in different ways. It's just how we find what gives us pleasure, beyond just doing things that make us happy through an endorphin rush. Still, within our community, because of this spectrum of people and experiences, we have those who are bad faith actors and those who are trying to build a community. The bad faith actors are more visible sometimes, for whatever reason, and they start to become the representation of our community in a negative way, which creates fear in some people about who we are. Then, there are those of us who are trying to push for a better understanding, to show what works positively, to highlight how we build each other up. It's hard for people to see that in general, which is why I think we want to be more visible and show that things can go well with the right communication and right dynamics.

YOU CAN HAVE THESE ALTERNATIVE LIFESTYLES THAT STILL WORK WITH THE REST OF THE WORLD. **WE'RE NOT PUSHING OUR LIVES ON OTHER COUPLES OR FAMILIES THAT LIVE NEXT TO US. WE'RE NOT FORCING OUR NEIGHBORS TO FOLLOW OUR PERSONAL PROTOCOLS, BECAUSE THAT WOULD JUST BE WEIRD.** WE JUST LIVE OUR LIVES.

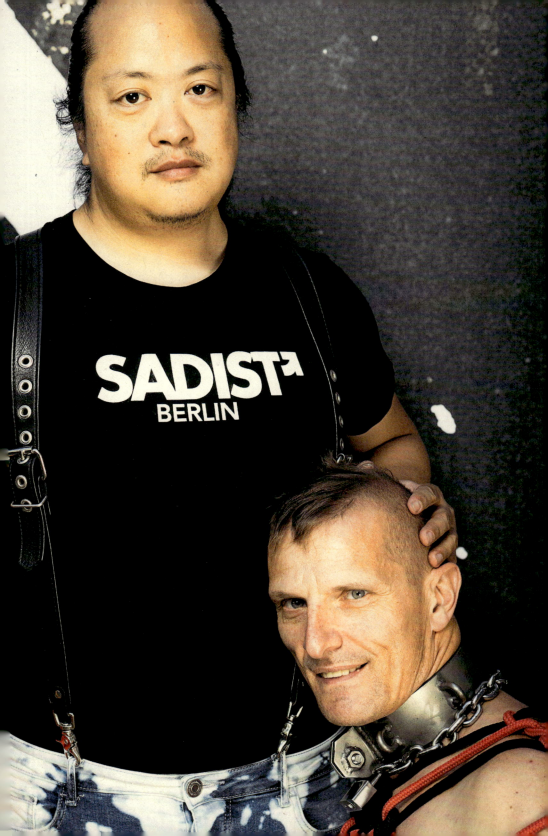

HOW DO YOU TRULY DEFINE WHAT IS NORMAL, WHAT IS STANDARD? FOR ME, KINK IS ACTUALLY MY NORMAL. IT'S WEIRD WHEN PEOPLE ASK, "WHAT IS YOUR KINK?" TO ME, MY KINK IS MY VANILLA.

When I was younger, I identified as bisexual because no other term really suited me. However, I dated so many trans people and still do to this day. People that are gender fluid, that are trans, or butch, or have some kind of gender nonconformity in them. That right there is my main type, if you will. And it isn't because they are trans. It is because the people who inhabit those bodies have done additional work around gender and identity that I found very attractive as a cis-presenting woman. So, when the term "pansexual" came around, I finally felt like a member of the LGBTQ+ community, because that little plus sign meant me. It identifies my experience more fully than bisexual ever did because I never believed in the binary construct of gender.

x x x

With age play, especially for trans people, it can be an opportunity to relive parts of childhood in the right gender, not necessarily the one assigned at birth. And that can be very healing. Kink can be therapeutic, but it is not therapy. I say this all the time. I see it being very therapeutic for some of my trans community members, because they are finally validated as a child in their gender.

KAREN MA'AM

PRONOUNS	She/Her	**RELATIONSHIP STATUS OR STRUCTURE**	Polyamorous
GENDER IDENTITY	Cisgender AFAB	**AGE**	51
SEXUAL ORIENTATION	Pansexual	**LOCATION**	Boca Raton, Florida, U.S.

WITH AGE PLAY, ESPECIALLY FOR TRANS PEOPLE, IT CAN BE AN OPPORTUNITY TO RELIVE PARTS OF CHILDHOOD IN THE RIGHT GENDER, NOT NECESSARILY THE ONE ASSIGNED AT BIRTH.

that. That took away all the restrictions I had put on myself. It wasn't about me pleasing this man. It was about him pleasing me, using me in a way I had consented to. To me, a very feminist thing to do. I had the choice and chose me. I chose my pleasure and my excitement and curiosity and had a shattering orgasm. I really screamed the whole house down. For me, it was the the first time I understood okay, kink is happening. I didn't have the words for it, but it was happening.

Physical touch is so important. It's important for growth, for mental health. It's important to feel yourself within the boundaries of your body, of where you exist. When I was a single mother of little ones, I wasn't intimately touched for years. My skin felt so hungry. I didn't know where I was in my body anymore. And most vanilla sex that is offered to women is self-serving, like a fast-food meal.

The depth and joy in a well-chosen kink experience can nourish and return you to your body, to feeling yourself and so much more.

LOLA

PRONOUNS	She/Her	**RELATIONSHIP STATUS OR STRUCTURE**	Married, in open relationship
GENDER IDENTITY	Fem	**AGE**	███
SEXUAL ORIENTATION	███	**LOCATION**	Germany/The Netherlands

For me, my kind of kink is very feminist. I identify as a Switch with a capital S.

There has to be fun involved. After all, if you can't laugh with a sex partner, then what are you doing?

Kink is a very caring and nurturing exchange for me. I love to care and feed. Cooking for someone is the ultimate form of domination. I mean, you prepare something that goes into someone else's body! Just like topping a sub, it takes knowledge, skill, preparedness, creativity, the right setting and you need to be able to adjust to the individual needs of the recipient. If someone doesn't eat my (kind of) food, I can't have sex with them. If they only eat fast food, I completely lose interest, no matter how hot they were to me before. Kink, just as food, nurtures the body and the soul. If you do it right, that is.

Sex isn't necessarily included in kink for me. It can distract me from what I am most interested in. For me, it's the person, their reactions, their emotions. Their face before and after. Seeing this is something I did, something I managed together with them. I can breathe, smell and taste their emotions. That's more intimate to me than sex.

I grew up Catholic, so I know a thing or two about role play, rules, service, and power exchange. There was a lot of gaslighting going on. Do I feel what I feel? Am I allowed to feel what I feel? So now I really enjoy seeing raw emotions, witnessing them. I have an informed choice! Pain can be a good thing. I have the power to say YES or NO. And I can choose who I give power over me or share an experience with.

I am allowed to take responsibility or to give myself over into caring hands for a set period of time within previously communicated restrictions. Knowing this was a big thing. It was such a huge eye opener.

So that's where my emotional voyeurism comes from. It's not just me who has feelings, but others do too. I'm like a kid in a candy shop when I see other people's emotions in a BDSM context. I totally enjoy and rejoice in the reality of it. That's my personal emotional voyeurism.

In my early 20s, I had a long-distance relationship with someone I met online. We chatted a few days, then moved on to telephone calls, falling asleep next to each other on the phone at night. Within two months I got on a plane to see him.

We had sex the first night. It just fit. He tied me to the bed. I already had kids and been single for two years, but it was the first time in my life I orgasmed through sex. And the reason for this: I could not run away. If somebody had called me at that moment, I wouldn't have been able to go. There was no way for me to get away. So, I was free to allow myself to be in it. I was able to let go. Simple as

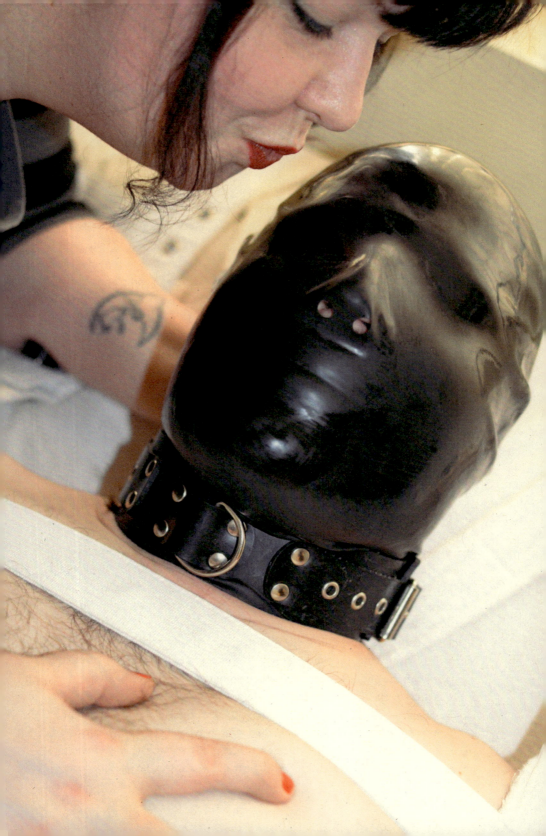

KINK IS A VERY CARING AND NURTURING EXCHANGE FOR ME. **I LOVE TO CARE AND FEED.** COOKING FOR SOMEONE IS THE ULTIMATE FORM OF DOMINATION. I MEAN, YOU PREPARE SOMETHING THAT GOES INTO SOMEONE ELSE'S BODY!

other people but I've never really thought it was a real … From that point forward, it was no longer something I had to endure. It was something to ride the wave of. Since then, I've been able to just exhale and it is mind blowing.

RIPTIDE

PRONOUNS	He/Him	**RELATIONSHIP STATUS OR STRUCTURE**	Boy to a Leather Daddy
GENDER IDENTITY	Male	**AGE**	54
SEXUAL ORIENTATION	Gay	**LOCATION**	Chicago / California, U.S.

I started really playing around when I was 19, with my first sexual encounter. I had fantasies about, and an attraction to, guys who were bigger and stronger than I was, which at the time, was not that hard. I was 125 pounds, skinny. The very first time I had sex with somebody, it was with a big, muscular guy taller than I was. He was about twice my weight at roughly 250 pounds. And he tied me up and had his way with me.

    He found out right before he was about to penetrate me that I was a virgin. I was tied up bent over his bed. And he had me gagged. He asked me, "When was the last time you were really fucked by a man?" Through the gag I said, "I haven't been." So, he lined up his big dick and he slammed it all the way up. And I screamed. It hurt, and I was in heaven … That's how he introduced me to sex. It was everything that I had fantasized about. It hurt and that triggered the pain reflex that I love. I was lucky to get what I truly wanted, but it also made things kind of hard, because everything gets compared to the first time. Really, it was about the control, the loss of it. My first love was bondage; it has always been a huge thing. The more immobilizing the better. I had to deal with whatever came, whether it be pain or something else. Pain and bondage just had to be there.

x x x

From that point forward, it was no longer something I had to endure. It was something to ride the wave of. Since then, I've been able to just exhale and it is mind blowing.

The first time I ever broke getting flogged was life changing. Before that, scenes with a top flogging me was something I had to endure or to get to what was next. But, then, I was with someone and they had me on a cross. And I was blindfolded. And during the flogging I was all tensed up, flexing my back just to take the hits. At one point, I remembered to just breathe, exhaling and just relaxing into the cross. That was the first time that I got that break, that flood of emotion. And even though I was blindfolded, I remember bright white lights and I just bawled out all that stress, all that we hold in. I don't know how long we went on before I got taken down, and I just wrapped my arms around the man as he held on to me. That was changing. That changed me. That was a moment when I was like: *Oh, I heard about this from*

IT WAS EVERYTHING THAT I HAD FANTASIZED ABOUT. **IT HURT AND THAT TRIGGERED THE PAIN REFLEX THAT I LOVE.**

I feel that there is a demand for the visuals, the superficial visuals and style of kink. There always has been. Every fashion designer, every once in a while, dips their toe into the dominatrix look. But the practice of kink, the ethics, the knowledge, the principles of consent and negotiation, all this stuff that is in my mind important, is so much harder to be expressed. And I think that's where kinksters are in a precarious state, where we're liked up to a point. And then the moment we go over the line, which we didn't even know was there, or was moved, is when we get smacked down.

It's like Gayle Rubin said, way back in 1984. She wrote about "the magic circle." And inside the circle is what's allowed in terms of sexual behavior. And outside of that circle is what's not protected, that portion of kink which is not a part of the privileged lifestyle. And so when I look at something like *Fifty Shades of Grey*, what I see is that boundary has shifted in one area, that it's extended to allow BDSM play, but also that the circle has contracted in other areas. So *Fifty Shades of Grey* gives us this image of kink that is hetero, monogamous, white, upper-middle class, aspirational. And if you're inside of that, if your sexual life is privileged, then you're allowed to do kink. But if you're of these other categories of people — if you're queer, if you're not monogamous, if you're not upper-middle class — then you're in trouble.

It's like, gays are okay, if you know they're white, middle class, and monogamous. And not too sexual. Not too kinky. Then they're allowed.

PETER TUPPER

PRONOUNS	He/Him/His	RELATIONSHIP STATUS OR STRUCTURE	Single
GENDER IDENTITY	Male	AGE	51
SEXUAL ORIENTATION	Straight	LOCATION	Vancouver, Canada

EVERY **FASHION DESIGNER,** EVERY ONCE IN A WHILE, DIPS THEIR TOE INTO THE DOMINATRIX LOOK. BUT **THE PRACTICE OF KINK,** THE ETHICS, THE KNOWLEDGE, THE PRINCIPLES OF CONSENT AND NEGOTIATION, ALL THIS STUFF THAT IS IN MY MIND IMPORTANT, IS SO MUCH HARDER TO BE EXPRESSED.

I am trans-masc. I had what I call my "slut summer" in 2020. Not the best time to have had a slut summer because of the pandemic, but that was the summer that my ex convinced me to be polyamorous. I slept with three cis guys during that time. None of them were particularly good. And that's when I realized T4T is all that I need. This abbreviation of "trans-for-trans" has evolved into a shorthand for a trans-centric politics of care, love, and solidarity. Not only as something sexual or romantic, but in the sense of: *We are trans people for trans people, and it's about community.*

It is what I crave in a relationship. My Sir is also trans-masc. Going to play parties, we tend to specifically watch trans couples play. T4T is a huge part of the way that I interact with kink. My Sir and I decided less than a week after the breakup with my former partner, that we wanted to be monogamous. The previous polyamory thing—we were very happy it happened because it gave us some really good perspective on relationships and the way that we view them. It just wasn't for us. I say that with a grain of salt. Because we now have a very dear friend who is another trans-masc person. He has a very dominant personality. And we've kind of entered this monogamish-voyeur situation where he watches me and my Sir fuck, he watches us kiss, and all of the things that we do together. He watches it happen and he gets off on it. We all really enjoy this dynamic together, because it's a self-created dynamic.

It's not polyamory because we don't touch him. He doesn't touch us. He has a partner completely separate from this. He has his own sub who just doesn't care to watch it. But it's very clearly not monogamy. We can't be fit into a box.

MOSS

PRONOUNS	He/Him	RELATIONSHIP STATUS OR STRUCTURE	Dominant/submissive
GENDER IDENTITY	Trans Man	AGE	▮▮▮
SEXUAL ORIENTATION	Gay	LOCATION	▮▮▮

**WE CAN'T
BE FIT
INTO
A BOX.**

I very recently made a decision that I've been wanting to make for the past few years — and that is to collar myself. I don't mean an actual dog collar. I recently bought a custom necklace that has my scene name on it … It's all about me loving myself. I am well aware that when I'm in vanilla spaces, like when I go to school or visit my family, I'm going to have to take it off. I'm well aware that if my boyfriend wanted to take a selfie with me, I would have to take it off. I am totally okay with having to constantly put it on and take it off.

With collaring myself, that's a promise I'm making to put myself first and it's okay if other people don't get it. I do think the kink community at large is still very unfamiliar with self-collaring. I think most people view collaring as a kinky equivalent to marriage. I personally disagree with that … Talking about collaring brings up a lot of mixed emotions for me. I even asked my significant other if he would mind if I wore my scene name necklace during sex, and he said it's totally okay. I wasn't asking him for permission. I just wanted to hear what he thought.

FELICITY AZURA

PRONOUNS	███	RELATIONSHIP STATUS OR STRUCTURE	Committed Relationship
GENDER IDENTITY	███	AGE	25
SEXUAL ORIENTATION	Bisexual	LOCATION	San Francisco, U.S.

WITH COLLARING MYSELF, THAT'S A PROMISE I'M MAKING TO PUT MYSELF FIRST AND IT'S OKAY IF OTHER PEOPLE DON'T GET IT.

The world of rubber and fetishism I knew slight hints about from an old documentary that would appear or a news item or an advert in a newspaper, but it always seemed very, very far away. And so it wasn't until my 20s that I could get myself down to London, and start really exploring the shops and the materials. I didn't have the bravery to also explore the community at that stage. It took another 20 years before I was able to get to my first event.

CATASTA CHARISMA

PRONOUNS	He	**RELATIONSHIP STATUS OR STRUCTURE**	
GENDER IDENTITY	Male	**AGE**	53
SEXUAL ORIENTATION	Heterosexual	**LOCATION**	United Kingdom

> I'd go visiting, soaring over landscapes and visiting the strange creatures and things out there. But it had to be kept secret. It had to be kept hidden.

I had an attraction toward stretch materials right from about the age of six. And I discovered, just as a kid exploring around the house, my mom's drawers of nylons and really tight hose and stockings. And I found this material fascinating. Stretch, open your hands, and see the webbing. Put it over the eyes and the world changed. You smelled differently, heard things differently. It was a transformation material. I was also born with a speech impediment. And I was highly frustrated in my inability to communicate properly to people, which made me angry. I was having speech therapy for years and years and years to try and overcome the issues.

So my life took two kinds of routes: One was that I was encouraged to draw, because then people get it: *Oh, it's a hippopotamus! That's what he's trying to say.* I could draw a hippopotamus, but I couldn't say hippopotamus. And then, the other route, was this discovery of the nylons. Which, when in that full encasement, it was like putting a baby in swaddling. I was quiet and I was at peace and could drift away in my own mind in a meditative state. And I'd go visiting, soaring over landscapes and visiting the strange creatures and things out there. But it had to be kept secret. It had to be kept hidden. There was a shameful aspect that it couldn't be expressed, that it couldn't be liberated.

So on one hand I got shaped as an artist to be able to express myself from a very young age. And then on the other hand, I had this medium that I wasn't allowed to explore, and that was being shaped more by the stigma. I had this dual kind of identity, which I began to develop into my teenage years. During that time, my evolution was ultimately leading toward rubber. I found the shiny aspects of rubber and PVC fascinating at a young age, but it was like it was the material of the kings and queens. They should be wearing this material that was so inaccessible from a place like this, an old mining village, the world where I grew up.

STRETCH, OPEN YOUR HANDS, AND SEE THE WEBBING. PUT IT OVER THE EYES AND THE WORLD CHANGED. YOU SMELLED DIFFERENTLY, HEARD THINGS DIFFERENTLY. IT WAS A TRANSFORMATION MATERIAL.

It prefers it.

It is deeply important to its entire being.

It means I or me.

It has never thought of itself as a man. It is not trans.

It still has the body of a man. It is an enslaved man.

It became a slave in 1999.

It says slavery underlies its entire life.

It didn't have this language when it was younger.

It was always it, though.

It volunteered.

It became a priest.

It believes service is all there is.

It knows that it is a service animal.

SLAVE SLIME

PRONOUNS	It/It/Its	RELATIONSHIP STATUS OR STRUCTURE	Owned Slave
GENDER IDENTITY	Male	AGE	72
SEXUAL ORIENTATION	Gay	LOCATION	Washington State, U.S.

IT PREFERS IT

It may be old news to some, but I really want people to know that the desire for intensity of experience in a variety of different kinds is not always derived from unhealthy places within the self. There is a lot of healthy, powerful, intense stuff that comes from deep within. Our whole life experience is a part of it. Kink is no more or less influenced by our hurts and pathologies than what gets called "vanilla" sex. Even though I'm aware of many folks who use kink as a way to heal themselves and work through a variety of things, and that's amazingly good, the same can be said about intimacy of any kind, or sexuality of any kind. I think pathologizing kink is the thing that bothers me the most.

IVO DOMINGUEZ, JR.

PRONOUNS	He/Him/His	RELATIONSHIP STATUS OR STRUCTURE	Married, Polyamorous
GENDER IDENTITY	Male	AGE	65
SEXUAL ORIENTATION	Queer	LOCATION	Georgetown, Delaware, U.S.

THE DESIRE FOR INTENSITY OF EXPERIENCE IN A VARIETY OF DIFFERENT KINDS IS NOT ALWAYS DERIVED FROM UNHEALTHY PLACES WITHIN THE SELF. **THERE IS A LOT OF HEALTHY, POWERFUL, INTENSE STUFF THAT COMES FROM DEEP WITHIN.**

> And because I so value someone using a safeword, my first reaction to them doing so is: "Thank you for taking care of yourself."

favorite things is to have somebody use a "pre" safeword. In other words, let's say I'm doing a flogging, and it's getting really hard, and it's getting close to their edge. I encourage people to say, "You know, ma'am, I'm not sure how much more of this I can take." It doesn't mean I have to stop, but it gives me the choice to back off and change what I'm doing, or continue and push them to their safeword. I love that because then I understand where their limits are. And I get that charge of: *I'm going to push you anyway, and get you there.* And because I so value someone using a safeword, my first reaction to them doing so is: "Thank you for taking care of yourself."

MARILYN HOLLINGER

PRONOUNS	She/Her	**RELATIONSHIP STATUS OR STRUCTURE**	Married, Master/slave
GENDER IDENTITY	Woman	**AGE**	61
SEXUAL ORIENTATION	Lesbian	**LOCATION**	San Francisco Bay Area, California, U.S.

When we talk to people about the nature of our relationship, that's how we talk about it, as a consensual granting of authority. We came out to our rabbi about our relationship, and we never used the words Master and slave. It's not about shying away from the words "Master" and "slave," but we understand the social context that makes those words difficult. However, I have yet to find a term that describes the totality of what we do. A lot of very smart people have been thinking about this for a very long time but have yet to come up with something better. People use owner / property and other terms like that, but I find that to be impersonal, and my slave is a person. I'm not judging that at all, but owner / property doesn't do it for me. Rio claims her slave identity. I don't dictate that; she uses that term. However, many people on their badges at events will say "slave Sammy" or whatever. And Rio does not. She uses "Rio, Marilyn's slave" because her primary identity is Rio and her being a slave is important, which is why it lives on the badge. But it's not her title.

x x x

Safewords keep me from harming anybody, so they're my bumpers. When I play with somebody new, I always push them to say their safeword, because I need to know that they will do that when needed.

When I do BDSM, I always play with safewords because for me part of my topping is about letting go, and safewords provide me safe boundaries. I live in a world where I have to hold myself in check a lot of the time, just being in the world, because my personality is big and controlling and that is often not socially acceptable. It's not okay to top a room without consent, for example. In interactions at work, I have to constantly make the box small. In more sexually charged environments, in kink or BDSM spaces, it's a way that I can be really big and strong and controlling. Safewords keep me from harming anybody, so they're my bumpers. When I play with somebody new, I always push them to say their safeword, because I need to know that they will do that when needed. Because if they don't, I could really damage them physically, emotionally, whatever. So I do a lot of negotiation and I insist on safewords. I make it very clear that I'm counting on them to keep me safe by doing that — because nothing would hurt me more than to actually damage somebody through my actions. One of my

Kink is anything that is outside of mainstream sexuality: So heterosexual, missionary, no toys; that very tiny little box that most of us don't fit in. I think most people do kink, whether they know it or say it. The degree to which they do it of course wildly varies. But I think most people are outside that little box. The kink community is about people who are open about what they do, educating themselves and others, and keeping everybody safe.

x x x

My particular kinks include leather, BDSM, and M/s (Master/slave). The values and the culture of the leather community — integrity, transparency, and humility — have really become my core personal values. For me, they are completely integrated in my life. Being a leader in the leather community has made me live those things. And I feel obliged to tell people the truth about how our community works. When I teach about BDSM or M/s for community groups, human sexuality classes, and in other venues, one of the first things I ask is how many of you have read *Fifty Shades of Grey* or know about it? And then I say now you want to take everything you've learned there and throw it out the window, because that's fiction and let me tell you the truth. What you read there was unsafe and was not consensual, and that's not how you do this stuff ethically. Kink is intentional and it's healthy and it's joyous. Kink is facilitating your journey into self-discovery, a sort of self-actualization. Kink is not therapy, but it is therapeutic.

The M/s aspect of my kink is how I define a specific way of interacting between me and my slave, Rio. However, when I first brought up my desires with Rio, I did not say, "I want you to be my slave." I said I wanted her to wear my collar. I did not use the word slave initially. For me, it was about relationship ownership, relationship responsibility, and her giving authority to me. In our relationship, where I have total control in many, many ways, Rio has the obligation — not the right, but the obligation — to share issues with me. She's obligated to tell me what she believes the impact of something will be on her.

KINK IS NOT THERAPY, BUT IT IS THERAPEUTIC.

I think that the way that kink has really influenced me is in my confidence and to really talk about what I'm thinking. When I first entered the kink scene in the UK, when I was 21, and still growing up, I had quite a lot of negative opinions about myself. I thought I was a very weak person. I thought I was a coward. I was scared a lot of the time. And kink taught me that I am so strong. I am not in any way a coward. I can be incredibly brave. And I went into situations and scenes and types of play in my early 20s that just changed that opinion of myself. That was enormous for me.

There was a scene that I participated in, where I had to cross London on my own to go to a group scene — a takedown-and-torture scene. I had to really have a lot of nerve to go through with that scene. And the people around me, who were much older and more experienced, were completely blown away by the fact I was able to do this at 21. That was just one of many scenes with those partners. I'm actually still with one of those partners today, 20 years later.

On the flip side, when I first moved to the San Francisco Bay Area in 2016, I was assaulted by a prominent member of the scene. He's gone on to be accused of assault by numerous people. I've not really publicly spoken about it because it scared me away from the scene for six years. And I only came back last year. In terms of cautionary tales, I think that shows how important community is because I see other people now coming out with their stories of assault within the scene. And they have amazing community support. And I wish I'd had that. So I want to try and help other people have that.

JESSAMY BARKER

PRONOUNS	They/She/He	RELATIONSHIP STATUS OR STRUCTURE	Polyamorous
GENDER IDENTITY	Genderqueer	AGE	42
SEXUAL ORIENTATION	Bisexual	LOCATION	Santa Cruz Mountains, California, U.S.

KINK TAUGHT ME THAT I AM SO STRONG. I AM NOT IN ANY WAY A COWARD. I CAN BE INCREDIBLY BRAVE.

crescendo. We were literally coming together in ecstasy, and having this emotional experience, with some people crying, and some people laughing. And at the end, everybody naturally comes down to this wonderful, low, kind of chill space. In the background, there are people drumming, there are people kind of holding space, people making sure everybody's okay.

    This experience was very significant for me in so many ways. It taught me how resilient I was. If I can do this, I can get over myself and whatever I'm feeling, and take my meds, and go back to work, and do my thing. If I can do this ritual, then I can do so much more ... I felt really connected to everything and felt stronger as an individual. I felt more compassionate as an individual. I felt more empowered as an individual. I felt like a badass as an individual. Because I fuckin' did that.

x x x

One thing that I want non-kinksters to take away is this: If you have a kinky friend, that's a friend you want to have with you when the shit hits the fan, like when the zombies come, during end-of-the-world shit. You want to have a kinky friend with you, because they're going to know how to tie a fucking knot. They're going to be able to transform all kinds of things to do stuff that they weren't really meant to do. We are resourceful motherfuckers.

KOKI VIETO

PRONOUNS	He/Him	RELATIONSHIP STATUS OR STRUCTURE	▇▇▇▇▇▇▇▇
GENDER IDENTITY	Cis-Male	AGE	46
SEXUAL ORIENTATION	Queer	LOCATION	San Francisco, U.S.

I FELT MORE **COMPASSIONATE** AS AN INDIVIDUAL. I FELT MORE **EMPOWERED** AS AN INDIVIDUAL. I FELT LIKE A **BADASS** AS AN INDIVIDUAL.

When you think of a hose and there's a kink in it, you know, it's just not straight. There's a little bit of a texture to it.

x x x

My first hook suspension is one experience that stands out to me as really transformative. When I became HIV-positive around 2007, I felt a lot of guilt, a lot of fear, a lot of anger. I felt physically non-viable. I had lost a lot of weight. I just wasn't feeling like a really healthy human being at the time. As it happens, a leather club I belong to sometimes has a Winter Solstice hooking ritual, and I was invited. I wasn't sure if I should go given my HIV status. I didn't want to mess up anybody's experience. I didn't know how to be safe for myself and other people. But I went to the ritual, and I shared my concerns with the host: "I just learned I am HIV-positive earlier this year, and I'm feeling these emotions and I'm feeling this way physically, too." He knew exactly what I needed to hear:

Our bodies are really resilient. Your body's resilient. You're strong. You would be surprised just how strong you are. I can tell you right now that physically you're going to be able to do it. As far as your concerns around HIV, as you can see, we have gloves, we have ample materials to keep this as safe as possible. A lot of the people here have certifications in this stuff. I encourage you to use the holes that we're going to put in your body to let out all that shame, to let out all that guilt, to let out all that emotion in your body, and just go for the ride. Now, we're here to feel something amazing. We're here to feel, to transcend, to have this beautiful experience in the group. I really feel like you could get something out of this. But it's your choice.

I got the hooks on my chest and back, and enjoyed the ritual. It is one of those experiences that's not what you think. I didn't think it was going to be so spiritual, so connecting to the earth, so connecting to other individuals on a really deep level. Part of the ritual was to put strings on your hooks, and you hand the strings to another participant, and they pull the strings. And you have their strings, to pull them. Sometimes you connect with them, and sometimes you pull away, and it was just this act of complete trust. Also, there are chemicals being released throughout our bodies, a lot of wonderful, natural chemicals that we make when we have pain. So everyone is feeling the combination of all these endorphins, these emotions, and this experience all together, and it comes to a

I GOT THE HOOKS ON MY CHEST AND BACK, AND ENJOYED THE RITUAL. IT IS ONE OF THOSE EXPERIENCES THAT'S NOT WHAT YOU THINK. **I DIDN'T THINK IT WAS GOING TO BE SO SPIRITUAL,** SO CONNECTING TO THE EARTH, SO CONNECTING TO OTHER INDIVIDUALS ON A REALLY DEEP LEVEL.

I know that I, personally, have learned a lot about the importance of being willing to say what you need as soon as you know it, in as clear a way as you possibly can. I've also learned, bizarrely, that I need more alone time than I usually think I do. I think we've both become much more attentive and patient partners — with each other and with others. But I was surprised to find that the aspect of my life that polyamory has influenced most is my platonic friendships. I treat them with so much more reverence and importance than I ever used to. I'm a more thoughtful friend, more generous with my time and my love, and that has been a tremendous gift. With an abundance of romantic love in my life, I'm able to see so clearly how special and important that kind of relationship is. Those, often, are the relationships in our lives that last the longest.

> I was surprised to find that the aspect of my life that polyamory has influenced most is my platonic friendships.

REBECCA ORCHANT | SEAN GARDNER

PRONOUNS	She/Her | He/Him	**RELATIONSHIP STATUS OR STRUCTURE**	Polyamorous
GENDER IDENTITY	▮▮▮▮▮▮	**AGE**	40 | 42
SEXUAL ORIENTATION	Queer	**LOCATION**	Provincetown, Massachusetts, U.S

If someone had asked me to define kink even five years ago, I would have told them I absolutely have no business being the one to do it. In fact, even now, I balk at the thought: *Who am I to say? Do I participate enough? Am I really invested in kink enough to speak about it?* I wonder if a lot of folks have this reservation.

I've never felt like either of us belonged to any kink or fetish community. We both enjoy elements of sensation play, impact play, toying with power exchange, and tend to think about sex as an arena for discovery, both of ourselves and our partners. Investing in polyamory in earnest for the last (oh wow) almost 10 years has given us a lot of fodder (and several different personality types) to find new desires, new curiosities, and new favorites. I guess, to be honest, that the more sex I have outside of "the norm," the less I'm really even sure what is kinky and what isn't. Five years ago, I would have said that an evening devoted to being tied up and spanked was definitely kinky, but at this point, I have a hard time imagining that most folks don't eventually try that or something like it? Is fucking someone with a strap-on kinky? Does that do a disservice to both kink and sex with a strap?

We are not a straight couple, although we often appear to be that to folks who don't know us. This is often very annoying, but occasionally affords us a very useful ability to code-switch between environments. The more queer sex we participate in, the more alienating it feels to be clocked as straight, and the more gleefully free of what does and doesn't constitute sex we feel beholden to. We came to polyamory in the first place as totally inexperienced, but very well-read nerds — we love research. But reading every book you can find can never prepare you for the first time you fall in love with another partner, the first time you realize you won't be able to meet a need for someone you love, or the moments when you wonder why you're even living like this in the first place. For us, living non-monogamously has never been about wanting to have any one specific version of it — a triad, separate relationships, only casual sex — but rather to be able to meet other people where they are in their lives, to see if our desires fit theirs, either together or separately, and to be able to love who we happen to love, unencumbered by the structure and expectations of traditional monogamy.

> **The more queer sex we participate in, the more alienating it feels to be clocked as straight**

WE ARE NOT
A STRAIGHT
COUPLE,
ALTHOUGH
WE OFTEN
APPEAR TO
BE THAT
TO FOLKS
WHO DON'T
KNOW US.

> There were people in America in bars, having fundraisers for me, and sending me hundreds of dollars.

I started to fundraise for my top surgery and put a GoFundMe out. I wasn't expecting anybody to engage with it. I did it in my title year as International Mr. Bootblack but I really wasn't expecting it to really touch people. I felt kind of guilty doing it. I was like, I should be able to navigate this on my own. I'm an adult; I shouldn't need to fundraise. But the cost was just outside of my limit of what I could afford. And we raised all the money in about three-and-a-half months. By the time I went back to IML (International Mr. Leather), I had all of the money I needed for my top surgery. There were people in America in bars, having fundraisers for me, and sending me hundreds of dollars. And my IML brothers, and the community as a whole, transcend place and location. That's something that I think we need to cherish and keep on nurturing.

ALISTAIR LEATHERHIRAETH

PRONOUNS	He/Him	**RELATIONSHIP STATUS OR STRUCTURE**	Daddy/Dom/Master, slave to one
GENDER IDENTITY	Trans Masculine	**AGE**	58
SEXUAL ORIENTATION	Bisexual	**LOCATION**	Wales, U.K.

The things that I practice in my life come with connection. It's connection between people. It's that energy exchange that you have with each other. That's what bootblacking is for me, that's what wielding a whip is for me. It's the connection with the person. That's the most important thing for me. My leather path is kind of spiritual, in a way. I guess, to me, my leather path was part of self-development and learning and growth. For me, that goes alongside spiritual growth and those connections with people are part of my spirituality.

Energy is something that's inherent that we all have. It's whether you choose to tune into it or not. And to me, that's what makes me want to play with somebody. That's what makes me want to give them a bit of an extra shine and, you know, have some play in the chair with them. That's what makes me want to be on the end of the whip or pain or whatever it is that we're using. It's not really, I suppose, what some people call "chemistry." I think it's more than that. I think it's a very vulnerable and honest part of yourself that is relating to another person.

x x x

I've learned where service actually comes from. It's not just a submissive thing. Dominants serve as well. They serve in different ways. And service is something that is very dear to my own personal relationships. There is an element of service in everything I do and in everything that my boys give me.

x x x

I was always Daddy. Even before I started my transition journey, I was always accepted in the kink community as Daddy or Sir. And that was never questioned. Nobody ever said to me, "But you're a woman." Nobody ever questioned my pronouns or anything. It was accepted, and it was my space to feel safe. It was my space where I felt myself.

x x x

I'VE LEARNED WHERE **SERVICE** ACTUALLY COMES FROM. IT'S **NOT JUST A SUBMISSIVE THING. DOMINANTS SERVE AS WELL.** THEY SERVE IN DIFFERENT WAYS.

Yes, we're very safety conscious in Europe. But the concept of absolute safety doesn't exist over here. So we do the *RACK* thing: Risk Aware Consensual Kink. We try to educate everybody about the risks involved and it's their choice whether to take them or not.

And of course, sometimes you have the drunk guy wielding a nine-foot, single-tail whip all over the room and hitting anything but his sub. I just take that thing away and throw him out. It is common sense. But safety in a kink setting means knowing a lot. Safety in a kink setting is having skills. Safety in a kink setting is being aware of the risks. It's now this far more absolute thing in the U.S.: *This is a risk, so you're not allowed to take it*. This is something we do differently in Europe.

SVEN

PRONOUNS	He/Him	RELATIONSHIP STATUS OR STRUCTURE	Married
GENDER IDENTITY	Male	AGE	63
SEXUAL ORIENTATION	Heteroflexible	LOCATION	Vienna, Austria

SAFETY IN A KINK SETTING IS **HAVING SKILLS.** SAFETY IN A KINK SETTING IS BEING **AWARE OF THE RISKS.**

I FIND KINK TO BE **WEIRDLY WHOLESOME.** KINK TO ME IS LIKE PLAY.

LADY V

PRONOUNS	She/Her	**RELATIONSHIP STATUS OR STRUCTURE**	Hierarchical Polyamory, Master/slave, Daddy Dom/little girl
GENDER IDENTITY	Trans Female	**AGE**	31
SEXUAL ORIENTATION	Pansexual	**LOCATION**	Salem, Oregon, U.S.

I find kink to be weirdly wholesome. Kink to me is like play. All of us are mostly theater nerds, and this is just like adult theater in real life.

x x x

> being cow to me is like this symbolism of motherhood

I am a human cow. Being a human cow has always really appealed highly to me. There's a lot of elements of autonomy specifically, that have always called to me. HuCows and cow-prints got really big a few years into the Trump administration, with autonomy loss in women and gay people, queer people, and trans people. And in some ways cow print is very much a way of reclaiming our autonomies, because so often we look at cows and we just see animals, cattle. And it's so much more powerful than that. To me, being a cow is this really well-rounded thing. It's a spectrum of anywhere from: *I am a cow-cubus and I'm gonna lock you into a jail cell and make you feed off me. And that's the only way you're gonna get out of my jail cell, you're gonna become my thrall.* Or I can like forced breeding scenes where I'm restrained and bound and I've got a milking machine on, and I've been forced to moo in front of an audience, while getting sodomized at the same time. It's a very wide spectrum, and it's something that I really love deeply. I actually teach a class on HuCow and bovine play. In early 2023, I was actually able to unveil the HuCow pride flag just to bring more awareness because we don't talk a lot about cows in the community, especially our male bovines and our gender expansive bovines. We try to bring light to everyone. I love my farmers and ranchers. It's a kink that speaks so deeply to me, because it ultimately comes from a place on the spectrum of care and love: *I want to see you grow ... or you're a piece of meat, and I'm gonna beat you and tenderize you.*

> and that's what I want to do: raise people and raise community.

But being cow to me is like this symbolism of motherhood that I can't really have especially as a transgender woman. I can grow my community, I can grow the people around me, but I can't have my own children. But I can raise people, and that's what I want to do: raise people and raise community.

I AM A HUMAN COW.

My kink for spandex started at a very early age, maybe 7 or 8 years old, watching the *Mighty Morphin Power Rangers,* Dean Cain in *Lois & Clark: The New Adventures of Superman,* and *American Gladiators.* Growing up in Montana, in a very conservative Mormon household, I didn't understand what I was feeling or experiencing, but I knew it was something wonderful and exciting. Only when I got to college did I realize: *Oh, I'm turned on by this and it gives me sexual pleasure and fulfillment,* and I could feel comfortable exploring with other men. This fearless and shameless self-discovery continues to today in San Francisco, where I am a proud and out leather switch, bootblack, and spandex fetishist!

x x x

When it comes to consensual erotic hypnosis, one of the people that inspires me is HairyHypnotist from Amsterdam, who jokes that he programs computers during the day, and programs good boys at night. The most exciting thing he taught me about erotic hypnosis is that, as a Hypno Dom, I can get into a submissive's headspace and play however I want (with consent) with that erotic imagination. I like the freedom that hypnotism gives me to explore things that can be impossible to do in real life. For example, one of the first experiences I had as a hypnosis sub was becoming a dog, losing the ability to speak human words, and seeing the world in black and white. It was very thrilling!

SKY RUSSELL

PRONOUNS	He/Him	RELATIONSHIP STATUS OR STRUCTURE	Dom ("alpha") to a sub ("pig")
GENDER IDENTITY	Cis Male	AGE	38
SEXUAL ORIENTATION	Gay	LOCATION	San Francisco, U.S.

I CAN GET INTO A SUBMISSIVE'S HEADSPACE AND PLAY HOWEVER I WANT (WITH CONSENT) WITH THAT **EROTIC IMAGINATION.** I LIKE THE FREEDOM THAT HYPNOTISM GIVES ME TO **EXPLORE THINGS THAT CAN BE IMPOSSIBLE TO DO IN REAL LIFE.**

It's a pretty common joke that children's movies about talking animals help people become furries. I think it's easy to see how this could be true, because you're growing up and you're identifying with these very human-like animal characters. Of course it's going to be easy to see yourself as them. I think the same principle applies to other forms of media too, though. Our society is so averse to sex, yet we use it to manipulate people's emotions all the time. I think an unintended side effect of that is, a lot of things that weren't always sexual have become more widely sexualized. For me personally, one of the big ones was equating sex and danger: *Oh, no, they're all tied up because they're in danger. Oh, no, they've been slashed and now they've lost their shirt.* Think of all the horror movies where the sexy victim takes off their clothes right before they get murdered. It's easy to start connecting those two things together and before you know it you get excited by things like bondage or blood play … So I feel like I got introduced to kink through art and media a lot sooner than I got introduced to it as a thing real people did.

IAN

PRONOUNS	He/Him	RELATIONSHIP STATUS OR STRUCTURE	Partnered
GENDER IDENTITY	Male	AGE	35
SEXUAL ORIENTATION	Gay	LOCATION	California, U.S.

OUR SOCIETY IS SO AVERSE TO SEX, YET WE USE IT TO MANIPULATE PEOPLE'S EMOTIONS ALL THE TIME.

The advice I would give someone new to kink is one word: Observe. And don't just observe by simply watching other people do things. Observe your own feelings. Observe how what you're seeing and what you're hearing is hitting you. Because we're really just an entire community of people teaching other people from our own experience. It really is just about paying attention and finding the things that speak to you in a way that works for you. Just observe what you're feeling and what you're perceiving, and you'll know.

MASTER DEVYN STONE

PRONOUNS	He/Him	**RELATIONSHIP STATUS OR STRUCTURE**	Master/Owner
GENDER IDENTITY	Trans Man	**AGE**	33
SEXUAL ORIENTATION	Queer	**LOCATION**	Colorado Springs, Colorado, U.S.

Kink is authority transfer. Kink is conscious inequality in our relationships. And it's the idea that I can do whatever I want, as long as the person who I'm doing it with consents. It doesn't have to fit into any social idea of what a relationship or what a sex life or what interactions between two or five or 12 people has to be.

My breakfast is part of my kink. I sit down on my couch and my doll comes over and says, "What do you want for breakfast, Sir?" I tell her I want eggs and toast, and then it arrives with an adorable doll on her hands and knees, giving me my breakfast. Then, as I pass my property on the staircase, it gives me a little acknowledgement nod. That means: *I'm about to go to work and make money for you to pay your rent. I'll see you later.*

x x x

As a trans person, I never thought I could or would be recognized within the leather community as a man. But my path in leather was kind of paved with my experience as a military brat, and as a motorcycle club kid. So those traditions of earning your place, earning your rank really spoke to me. It was really important to me that the folks around me knew that this was one of my desires, and having them all tell me I'd earned serious recognition at the South Plains Leatherfest meant the world to me. South Plains is an event that shaped me as a kinkster and as a leatherman, but it's also an event that really harmed me. It was a pivotal moment for me, realizing and reclaiming, that this is a space where I had both extreme positives and also extreme negatives. This is an event that showed me I was a dominant. This is the place where I discovered that I wanted a submissive or a slave. This is also the place where I was in the parking lot, on my hands and knees, puking and screaming: "Why has God put me in this body? What did I do?" Understanding and holding these two extremes at the same time made me realize that my perseverance and my strength are one side of me, but my ability to continue forward, and what I want to do in this community, regardless of what obstacles might be thrown at me, are quite another side of me. Being recognized outside of myself, by the community, really meant something to me.

x x x

THE ADVICE I WOULD GIVE SOMEONE NEW TO KINK IS ONE WORD: OBSERVE. AND DON'T JUST OBSERVE BY SIMPLY WATCHING OTHER PEOPLE DO THINGS. OBSERVE YOUR OWN FEELINGS. OBSERVE HOW WHAT YOU'RE SEEING AND WHAT YOU'RE HEARING IS HITTING YOU.

There is no one specific, normal, right, sanctioned, good way to have sex. I know that from my own experience of having dug in and really taken possession of what turns me on. And what very specifically turns me on is group masturbation. I am now part of a community of people who enjoy this together. This led me to recognize that the whole standard narrative of conventional sexuality and "what's right" is a myth. There are all these ideals that we set up and we invest belief in, but those things don't actually exist. They are illusions. And when you break away from that and start to see people for the way human sexuality actually works, you start to appreciate people for being the individuals they are, for having a rich life under the hood. They may or may not be willing to share it, either intellectually or physically, but it's there. So kink has transformed my relationships with people on so many levels. I think that this transgressive streak is in most of us, if not all of us.

PAUL ROSENBERG

PRONOUNS	He/Him	RELATIONSHIP STATUS OR STRUCTURE	Married
GENDER IDENTITY	Male	AGE	65
SEXUAL ORIENTATION	Gay	LOCATION	Seattle, U.S.

THERE IS NO ONE SPECIFIC, NORMAL, RIGHT, SANCTIONED, GOOD WAY TO HAVE SEX.

THE WHOLE STANDARD NARRATIVE OF CONVENTIONAL SEXUALITY AND **"WHAT'S RIGHT" IS A MYTH.**

RÍO

PRONOUNS	He/Him	**RELATIONSHIP STATUS OR STRUCTURE**	Single
GENDER IDENTITY	Trans Masculine	**AGE**	39
SEXUAL ORIENTATION	Bisexual	**LOCATION**	Mexico City, Mexico

I tied him, then I understood that I had all the control. I think that changed the narrative for me, that sometimes in this world men have all the control, and for me it was very exciting to know that he couldn't touch me. I think that made all the difference, that I was in control, not him, a man. I tied him up, so he could not touch me. That makes the moment really funny for me.

There was also a moment that I let him take a little control, like for 10 seconds. And it was really strange because in that 10 seconds, he just started choking me, and it was a moment when I was like: *Okay, yeah, I also like to be in a submissive place*. But I knew that I had the control, so when I said that's enough, I just pulled him away, and he was really obedient. We just saw with our eyes that we had both been pleased. I tied him, I hit him with my flogger. And he enjoyed that I never let him have his ejaculation.

The way that he expressed all his frustration was in the way he choked me. But it was in that moment that it was really crazy for my mind, because I live in this country where a lot of women are killed because of these kinds of actions by a guy. For a second, I thought: *Oh my god, what I'm doing!* But when I realized that I had the control and I just told him so, and he understood, it was like, *Oh yeah, we can do this and play with this*. And it was really joyful. It was really a way to change this narrative of violence in this kind of country.

x x x

I am a survivor from torture in my country. I was a political prisoner 10 years ago. So, when these feminists ask me why I do this, saying I'm replaying violence, I say, *No, I know what violence looks like*. Because this body, as a woman, has already had a lot of violence, and I know how violence feels and looks. I know that doing this practice has nothing to do with that because when we have kink play, we are talking, we are listening to each other. We are taking care of each other, and in other practices I have never felt so secure and so caring about the other person, or the other person about me. That's everything.

NO, I KNOW WHAT VIOLENCE LOOKS LIKE. BECAUSE THIS BODY, AS A WOMAN, HAS ALREADY HAD A LOT OF VIOLENCE, AND I KNOW HOW VIOLENCE FEELS AND LOOKS. I KNOW THAT DOING THIS PRACTICE HAS NOTHING TO DO WITH THAT BECAUSE WHEN WE HAVE KINK PLAY, WE ARE **TALKING**, WE ARE **LISTENING** TO EACH OTHER. WE ARE **TAKING CARE** OF EACH OTHER, AND IN OTHER PRACTICES **I HAVE NEVER FELT SO SECURE AND SO CARING** ABOUT THE OTHER PERSON, OR THE OTHER PERSON ABOUT ME. **THAT'S EVERYTHING.**

SO, YEAH, I FIND IT REALLY CHALLENGING TO ALWAYS BE THE ONLY ONE. **IT'S HARD, REALLY, AND EXHAUSTING TO BE CONSTANTLY PIONEERING.**

And I'm excited. If I'm honest, I'm really excited to finally have something that is grounded in actual experiences of actual folks who are practicing kink, and not some outsiders. It feels really important, because this is created from us, by us, with us.

x x x

With my first husband, I discovered I definitely wasn't submissive. It always makes me laugh and I tell the story quite frequently. He tried to dominate me, and all I could do was laugh and giggle! I couldn't take it seriously, this isn't something I can really get behind. Can I be of service? Absolutely. Can I be told what to do? No. I know myself really well and I know what I'm happy to do or not, and actually I'm not a very good follower. I enjoy telling people what to do. I fully hold my hands up to being a control freak. And this was really beautiful to discover with him. That's something that will stay with me, that I feel fortunate to have had such a really personal kind of entry into kink with someone who I adored and loved, and who loved and adored me back. And to realize, oh, yeah, I am really into pain. And I'm definitely a sadist and definitely a masochist. But you really can't tell me what to do.

CARITIA

PRONOUNS	▪▪▪	RELATIONSHIP STATUS OR STRUCTURE	▪▪▪
GENDER IDENTITY	Non-Conforming	AGE	51
SEXUAL ORIENTATION	Queer	LOCATION	Berlin, Germany

So, my reservations about this book project come from a place of being really, ecstatically happy that this project exists, but also acknowledging that the whole team guiding it is white. And I don't want to be tokenized as someone in this lifestyle.

I actually didn't really see anyone else in it for a really long time, anyone who looked like me, anyone who was into the same things as me for years, decades, actually. Then, when I did come across people, I recognized that there's a very frankly Americanized version of what kink is for them.

Just trying to establish myself in the kink world is hard. And then feeling like: *Is there enough representation, and do I need to make myself more visible so that other people can see themselves reflected? In this life? In this way of being?* So, yeah, I find it really challenging to always be the only one. It's hard, really, and exhausting to be constantly pioneering.

I still respect this project so much, but I really want to make my voice heard with regard to it. To not just glaze over it, but to really go deep. I really would love there to be lots of different representation within the project. But I understand also, there are some limitations because I understand that folks of color and Black folks aren't always able to be visible because they could lose everything. That's true of almost anyone who's in this field, but more so of folks of color, where our will and authority is undermined, our voices are left out. We're often excluded from decision making and policymaking and lawmaking.

We're the ones who are really affected. As a queer, marginalized person, and someone who's neurodiverse and someone who hasn't had the financial means to always get all of the education that I would like to get, there are certain things I had to do. And one of those things is to start sex work, unexpectedly, just to basically have some freedom and autonomy. So, I feel like it's really important for me to be part of the project, but I think it's also challenging for me to be maybe the only one — or potentially to think am I the only one? I don't think I will be. But I felt like it was really important for me to speak up and say, how I was feeling and why I was feeling that way and acknowledge it.

I think we're all doing the best job that we can do. But the reality is that more white folks can have access to creating such projects. There's not the funding to do something like this if we were an all-minority team ... So I'm really, honestly grateful that everybody would like for me to be involved in the project. I feel it is a really valuable one ...

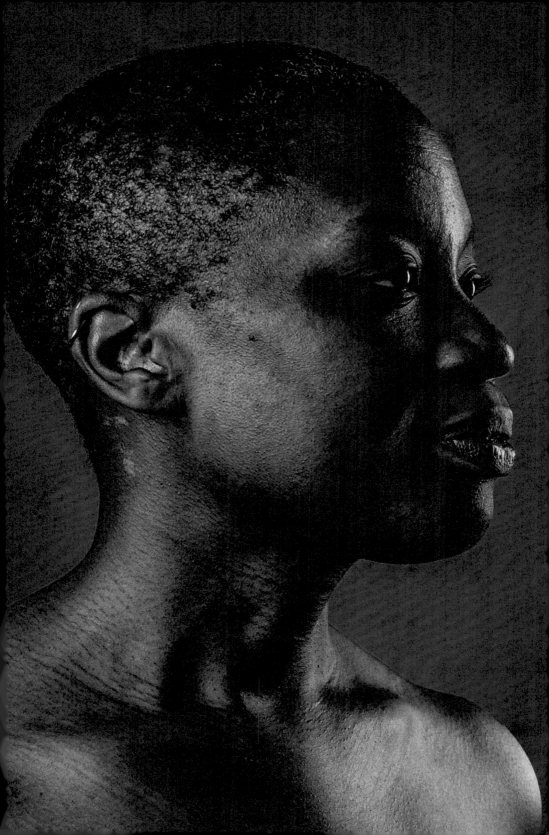

JUST TRYING TO ESTABLISH MYSELF IN THE KINK WORLD IS HARD. AND THEN FEELING LIKE: *IS THERE ENOUGH REPRESENTATION, AND DO I NEED TO MAKE MYSELF MORE VISIBLE SO THAT OTHER PEOPLE CAN SEE THEMSELVES REFLECTED? IN THIS LIFE? IN THIS WAY OF BEING?*

Since delving into kink, I learned a lot more about myself through my Sir. He uses kink scenes to help me open up various aspects about myself. During one session, out of habit I stifled a laugh. He noticed and then told me: "You don't need to do that. If you feel something in the moment, feel it. Vocalize how you feel to me." Coming from a Mexican background where machismo and stoicism are the norm, I often default to a stern face to mask what I'm feeling. My father often said, "Men do not cry or show weakness. You must always be strong." My Sir encapsulates the opposite of this through his encouragement to be vulnerable. Vocalizing how I feel shows trust in him and in myself to share in a space where I won't be told it's incorrect. Of course, the life experience he has along with his muscular arms to hold me helps. Now every time I see him, I let myself be vulnerable and share who I am.

FRED

PRONOUNS	He/Him	**RELATIONSHIP STATUS OR STRUCTURE**	▇▇▇▇▇▇
GENDER IDENTITY	Male	**AGE**	32
SEXUAL ORIENTATION	Gay	**LOCATION**	West Coast, U.S.

COMING FROM A MEXICAN BACKGROUND WHERE **MACHISMO** AND **STOICISM** ARE THE NORM, I OFTEN DEFAULT TO A STERN FACE TO MASK WHAT I'M FEELING.

MY SIR ENCAPSULATES THE OPPOSITE OF THIS THROUGH HIS **ENCOURAGEMENT TO BE VULNERABLE.**

dick, and I call my hole my pussy. The minute we say that, we understand each other. Everybody is allowed to be what they want once the heteronormative names for parts are removed. Think about it: so much of our culture is fixated on how we control and regulate our butts. *Where can we go to the bathroom? How do we cover our butts? When are we allowed to touch them? And for what purposes?*

And yet, butts are universal. Everybody has one. We are all equal. Shifting the focus to the butt gives us that equality, and it's a genderless equality. The butthole has no gender.

ALEXANDER CHEVES

PRONOUNS	He/Him/His	RELATIONSHIP STATUS OR STRUCTURE	▇▇▇▇▇▇▇▇
GENDER IDENTITY	Male	AGE	32
SEXUAL ORIENTATION	▇▇▇▇▇▇▇▇	LOCATION	Berlin, Germany

shameful. Fisting is not pre-approved. It's body modification. Many people still believe it ruins a butthole. "Ruin" is a strong word and depends on what someone considers ideal, but fisting does change a butthole. With every year of growth, I am changing. We are taught to be ashamed of well-worn bodies, even when they are well-worn by pleasure, and it took time for me to learn there is nothing shameful about modifying the body through sex. And I have.

I never thought I would learn so much about my identity, my friends, my deepest connections through fisting, but it has given me that. Fisting has led me to serious questions about my sexual orientation, even my gender. We associate sex and gender with our bodies, and through fisting, my body is being changed, so that puts everything into examination.

I'm into forced feminization, and I see this as tied to my fisting life. I am creating the hole I want and calling it a pussy. I have very little connection to my dick. I am really into wearing panties and lingerie. I understand this might be seen as trans curiosity, and I have thought about that quite a bit. I am grateful that fisting has given me the chance to examine my gender in a way I think few people do. I still feel cisgender, very male, but "male" is so malleable. I love how soft and receptive my male body can be. It does not absolve me of toxic masculinity — I still have privileges others don't — but being a hardcore fist bottom gives me a place to examine these things. Manhood to me feels both tender and powerful, strong and weak, and has nothing to do with a dick. It's as our trans family has said all along: parts don't matter. Gender is a play toy.

> When I wear women's clothes and get fist fucked, it honors me.

Forced feminization is often seen as a degrading act, by putting a submissive in his place, a lesser place, a female place. That is misogynistic, of course, except I don't feel lessened by it. Femininity is powerful. I feel empowered when and where I find it in me. When I wear women's clothes and get fist fucked, it honors me.

I have friends on similar journeys who are non-binary, and they have made me ask questions about myself. But for now, I'm male. Who knows about the future? At the same time, it's just clothes. I love that. That a piece of clothing can redefine me. I now fist with men, women, trans folk, and non-binary people. Everyone, basically. I play with anyone who understands fisting.

Fisting transcends gender, sexual orientation, bodies. It makes gender irrelevant. I play with a trans man in Berlin, where I live, and he calls his hand his

I didn't have language for it, but I had some sense of being kinky from a very young age. I took my toy figures and tied them up, or used tape from around the house to gag and restrain them, and I found it very powerful. So, it had all been building in me for some time.

When I had my first actual kink experience, I jumped into the deep end with a Sir. I learned and tried so much, so quickly. I was fascinated by all the terms and techniques. They felt both known and new at once. My first kink relationship, which happened in college, profoundly changed my life. From it, I learned how kink relationships can be good and bad at the same time — how kink can be healthy and life-saving even if the people you play with are not.

Fisting is my primary kink now, to the point that it is definitive of my sexuality. It's been the most rewarding journey of my sex life. I've done it for a decade and am pretty advanced at this point. But I still feel like a beginner, like I can do it better or go further. It's so integrated into me that I'm not sure I even consider myself a particularly kinky person. I just really love fisting. I don't need gear, or a scene, or anything special. Fisting is just my sex. Some people need a penis or certain body parts for sex. I need hands and forearms.

I originally encountered fisting in porn. At first, I was sure it was something I would watch online but never do. People like to watch things that scare them, and I thought fisting was just that: something akin to horror films or first-person shooter games, something I would experience indirectly via a screen but never do in real life. I felt that way for years.

Then I decided to try it, quite casually, which meant asking around and looking for someone to teach me. I felt like a lost puppy, out of my depth, intimidated by the idea of doing something I did not understand. The men I talked to either cautioned me against it or thought it was hot that someone so young wanted their ass stretched out. Wading through all the murky judgments and fantasies to find someone kind and patient was very hard, and I think it probably still is for beginners. I was afraid to explore my body because of what we are told: that we must use and enjoy our bodies in pre-approved ways and anything else is

> I was afraid to explore my body because of what we are told: that we must use and enjoy our bodies in pre-approved ways and anything else is shameful. Fisting is not pre-approved. It's body modification.

THE BUTTHOLE HAS NO GENDER.

So, at this party in July 2012, I was going to be suspended by my friends who had experience in tying up larger people. They worked in tandem, to put me in the ropes so it wouldn't take forever, and I was suspended from an octagon suspension rig. It was painted bright pink. And they had me sit in a chair since the rigging would take a little time.

    Once they had done all of their safety rigging, they told me to lean back and they would take the chair out from under me, and then they would slowly lay me down so I was facing up, fully horizontal. I didn't know until much later that I was literally six inches off the floor. I thought I was several feet above it, but your brain does not comprehend that.

    It made me want to cry. When they finally had gotten me horizontal, I stretched out my arms and just felt this energy come bursting out of my chest. And a friend of mine who's very energy aware, said the energy circled the room and just sucked back into me. My friend whispered into my ear, and I heard all these people cheering because they knew how important this was to me. And I'm just suspended there and feeling so loved by the people that were around me, and they said, "When you're ready, we'll let you back down."

    I don't remember doing anything the rest of the night. I don't remember the rest of what happened. But I cried periodically for about three days from this. And probably a couple of days more after that. I actually wrote about it and posted on FetLife. There have been so many people saying how wonderful it was to see because it's not typical. Larger people are not often in the pictures that you usually see, or who you normally see featured at a party in most places. And there were so many comments from people who were even smaller than me. They were like, *I have the courage now to ask for this. I didn't know it was possible.*

DOLLY

PRONOUNS	She/Her	RELATIONSHIP STATUS OR STRUCTURE	Single, Polyamorous
GENDER IDENTITY	Woman/Female/Femme	AGE	50
SEXUAL ORIENTATION	Lesbian	LOCATION	Columbus, Ohio, U.S.

WHEN THEY FINALLY HAD GOTTEN ME HORIZONTAL, I STRETCHED OUT MY ARMS AND JUST **FELT THIS ENERGY COME BURSTING OUT OF MY CHEST.** AND A FRIEND OF MINE WHO'S VERY ENERGY AWARE, SAID THE ENERGY **CIRCLED THE ROOM AND JUST SUCKED BACK INTO ME.**

MASTER KAYNE:

BY EXPLORING PAIN AND NEGATIVE EMOTIONS IN SAFE AND PLEASURABLE WAYS WE ARE ABLE TO RECLAIM THEM.

BAMBI:

KINK IS DIFFERENT FOR EVERYONE; FOR ME, IT'S A LIFESTYLE AND A LIFELINE. IT'S HOW I HANDLE TRAUMA, CHRONIC PAIN, AND MENTAL HEALTH ISSUES.

Master Kayne:

For me, BDSM is a journey of connection and growth. It's about creating a safe space where partners can explore their desires and sexuality. Kink has been transformative, teaching us empathy, communication, and mutual respect, and helping us build a foundation of trust and intimacy. By exploring pain and negative emotions in safe and pleasurable ways we are able to reclaim them and ultimately make us better for it.

Bambi:

Kink is different for everyone; for me, it's a lifestyle and a lifeline. It's how I handle trauma, chronic pain, and mental health issues. Kink can be anything and everything you want it to be — an incredible world where you can discover, accept, and explore yourself in ways you never thought possible. Before kink, I felt fundamentally flawed and ashamed of my desires. Discovering kink has allowed me to accept and understand myself. It's profoundly changed my life, giving me the strength to embrace who I am and navigate the world with confidence.

MASTER KAYNE | BAMBI

PRONOUNS	He/Him	She/They	**RELATIONSHIP STATUS OR STRUCTURE**	Dominant	submissive
GENDER IDENTITY	Cis Male	Genderfluid	**AGE**	36	26
SEXUAL ORIENTATION	Gynesexual	Queer	**LOCATION**	Adelaide, Australia

MASTER KAYNE:

BDSM IS A JOURNEY OF CONNECTION AND GROWTH. IT'S ABOUT CREATING A SAFE SPACE WHERE PARTNERS CAN EXPLORE THEIR DESIRES AND SEXUALITY.

When I first joined FetLife I put my role as "switch" because I like to hit people and I also like people to hit me and all that. And then I realized there was some kind of peer pressure. Switches haven't always gotten a lot of love. So, I thought: *I'm submissive then because I want for somebody to tell me what to do.* Then I started identifying as a slave. However, I would go to parties in New York when I was living there, and people would ask me to hit them and I loved it. So my friends would tease me: They were like, *Yeah, you know, you're really switchy.* I've really tried to push it down. But there's been a change recently. A few weeks ago, I went to the Master/slave Conference. And I said to myself: *You know what? Screw it. I'm gonna come out as me. I don't care what anybody thinks.*

The response was amazing. I have my leather vest, which I love, and it has "Girl" on it. And so I decided, I'm going to come out about this full force. I went to a vendor booth and asked: "Can you put *Ma'am* on my vest?" It just felt right. I'm kind of a leather auntie, because I have indigenous ancestry and being an auntie in the community is very important to me, a bit like a mentor to other people that are new coming in.

By the end of the conference, one of my Master friends was going around calling me "Uncle Stacey" because I had "Auntie" on my vest. And my friends were calling me "Sir Stacey," because I've been "Girl Stacey" for all these years. It is empowering. Whenever I have a moment of, *Oh, I can't do that,* the other part of me says, *Well, Sir Stacey could do it.*

STACEY DIANE

PRONOUNS	She/Her	RELATIONSHIP STATUS OR STRUCTURE	Slave to a Master; Switch, Ma'am
GENDER IDENTITY	Woman/Female/Femme	AGE	51
SEXUAL ORIENTATION	Queer, Bisexual	LOCATION	Washington, D.C. Area, U.S.

"CAN YOU PUT *MA'AM* ON MY VEST?" IT JUST FELT RIGHT. I'M KIND OF A LEATHER AUNTIE.

KINK IS

The problem I have is that I've always felt that I'm too kinky for the vanilla world, but a bit too vanilla for the kinky world. I'm a simple bondage lover, nothing more.

x x x

When I hit my late 20s, I tried to mold myself into what I felt like society wanted me to be, to live the heteronormative life of having the husband, two cats and a beautiful big house. But the problem was that I was never fulfilled in the bedroom in relation to my kink needs and desires due to the fact my husband wasn't naturally kinky. It is one of the main reasons we ended up getting a divorce.

After my separation, especially within the last couple of years, I've let my freak flag fly, shall we say. I've had so many kinky experiences and met so many amazing people whilst traveling the world. What's even better is I don't just look at the guys I have met as kinky friends, either. They're now good friends and it gives me comfort in the fact that they are all bondage lovers like me. It's a great community that I had missed being a part of during my relationship. A community that is full of love and acceptance.

Don't get me wrong, giving up my marriage was a risk and one of the hardest things I've ever had to do, because I was giving up so much of an amazing life I had with my husband. But during my travels I was able to fall for a few guys and that confirmed to me that I had made the right decision. And although I'm not in a relationship with any of them (not yet anyway), it gives me hope that I can have that feeling of everything I had with my husband, and then some, because my kink needs will actually be fulfilled at the same time. It's a feeling that I'd never experienced before and it gives me hope for the future. I am proud to be kinky and excited for what's to come.

GAZ

PRONOUNS	He/Him	**RELATIONSHIP STATUS OR STRUCTURE**	Divorced
GENDER IDENTITY	Male	**AGE**	35
SEXUAL ORIENTATION	Gay	**LOCATION**	Scotland, U.K.

I'VE ALWAYS FELT THAT I'M **TOO KINKY** FOR THE VANILLA WORLD, BUT A BIT **TOO VANILLA** FOR THE KINKY WORLD.

> kinky people can talk about anything and be okay with it.

I hang out with heterosexual kinksters more than with vanilla gay people. Someone asked me why, and I said: "Because kinky, straight people are more fun than the vanilla gay people." I think it's that kinky people can talk about anything and be okay with it. If someone's into diaper play, if someone's into fire play, or just a furry, kinksters are accepting of that. Vanilla people can tend to freak out more over alternative behavior.

x x x

I am a tickle bottom. I love electro-play. I like ice cubes. It's about sensation play. I don't like impact play. Most kinksters I know are very much into flogging and spanking. I am into other sensations.

x x x

Oh, god, yes, I have safe words! And I use the traffic signal colors: red, yellow, green. Yellow is important in slowing things down, but not stopping them. And green, if they have hit on something wonderful: *green!* I will get to know someone beforehand ... I vet people quite thoroughly and I think as you get to know them it is, in fact, a kind of a negotiation. They learn what you like and what your limits are. For me, a hard limit is: Do not touch the mustache! People want to do that.

CAPTAIN KINK

PRONOUNS	He/Him/His	**RELATIONSHIP STATUS OR STRUCTURE**	Single
GENDER IDENTITY	Male	**AGE**	70
SEXUAL ORIENTATION	Gay	**LOCATION**	Florida, U.S.

FOR ME, A HARD LIMIT IS: DO NOT TOUCH THE MUSTACHE!

AND, OH DO I LIKE TO FEEL LIKE THIS. YES, I HAVE ALSO WRITTEN MY STORIES, NOT IN A CELL IN THE 18TH CENTURY, BUT I HAVE WRITTEN MY STORIES ON MY COMPUTER, **WITH THE SAME PASSION FOR THE THINGS THAT ACTUALLY AROUSE ME,** EVEN IF THE MAJORITY OF PEOPLE WILL ABSOLUTELY DESPISE THEM AND BAN THEM. I DON'T CARE.

My kinkster side is usually more tied to media — books, literature, movies — than to actually getting together with people and going to a dungeon. Sometimes I have felt like I'm closer to de Sade than to normal, regular kinksters. Because I can imagine him, alone in a prison in 1784, writing *The 120 Days of Sodom,* hiding all these very arousing stories in his cell. I know that there are some philosophical interpretations, or moral interpretations, and Pasolini's horrible adaptation. But if you read the introduction, it says, *this is going to make you cum.* The stories are that level of perversion or passion for something to sexually arouse another. It's specifically written to be sexually arousing. And, oh do I like to feel like this. Yes, I have also written my stories, not in a cell in the 18th century, but I have written my stories on my computer, with the same passion for the things that actually arouse me, even if the majority of people will absolutely despise them and ban them. I don't care. I'm happy what I'm doing, with what I'm writing. This is important to me and I'm going to do it, anyway. I like that de Sade is still there, somewhere hidden in the BDSM letters. I feel very connected to that and to him.

x x x

Wearing diapers can be very impractical. One time, in Paris, I went to the movies in a diaper, and I drank too much cola. The diaper was way too full, and I was kind of stuck outside the cinema in Paris. The cinema had just closed, and there were no public bathrooms nearby. What could I do with this diaper? It's about to fall, and I have to take it off very carefully! I didn't want people to see me take off a diaper, from under my dress.

SAKURA

PRONOUNS	She/Her	RELATIONSHIP STATUS OR STRUCTURE	▮▮▮
GENDER IDENTITY	▮▮▮	AGE	▮▮▮
SEXUAL ORIENTATION	▮▮▮	LOCATION	▮▮▮

I remember my last diaper change, like actually by my mom, when I was quite young. I have some kind of picture in my head — kind of there, but not very clear. When I was around five or six years old, I think that was the time diapers disappeared from my house. I grew up as an only child, and I clearly remember trying to make a diaper out of paper. It made no sense and it didn't work, but I clearly remember trying to do that.

I don't necessarily get horny when I wear diapers. Many times, I don't become horny at all. When I put on diapers, it's something I just happen to like to do because it's comfortable, because it's nice.

x x x

> I don't necessarily get horny when I wear diapers. Many times, I don't become horny at all. When I put on diapers, it's something I just happen to like to do because it's comfortable, because it's nice.

KINK IS 123

I CAN IMAGINE HIM, ALONE IN A PRISON IN 1784, WRITING THE *120 DAYS OF SODOM,* HIDING ALL THESE VERY AROUSING STORIES IN HIS CELL.

HE CLOSED
THE TRUNK
AND GOT IN
THE FRONT
SEAT WITH
HIS FRIEND.

Then he kicked me. And he said, "When you're ready, come back out." And he went back to the bar. I'm sitting in the handicap stall. Total endorphin rush. And I go back out, he took off the collar, and that was it. No goodbye, no nothing. And I walked back to the Eagle where my car was, totally flying. I'm still friends with this person. I was very, very lucky in a number of different ways. But it also changed the way that I looked at things.

I loved it. I absolutely loved being in that situation, that scenario. The way that my Sir handled me was the first time somebody had physically been in charge of me. It is what I wanted and needed.

> Total endorphin rush. And I go back out, he took off the collar, and that was it. No goodbye, no nothing.

DAVE

PRONOUNS	He/Him	RELATIONSHIP STATUS OR STRUCTURE	Married
GENDER IDENTITY	Male	AGE	58
SEXUAL ORIENTATION	Gay	LOCATION	Oakland, California, U.S.

I came out late as gay and into kink, and in a therapy session, to remove my fear of kink, my therapist had me go to the San Francisco Eagle for just 15 minutes to get used to being in a gay kink environment. This was in the late 80s, so it was still very traditional, old-guard leather. Dealing with HIV was around, and AIDS was around. So, it was a very interesting time. But the experience — and it was really my first experience — was very good. I was lucky because it was with somebody who was not dangerous, let's just say. He could have been, given what I am going to share. But, truly, everything happened because I consented to it, even if passively.

The first time — or maybe like the fifth time — I went to the Eagle satisfying this assignment, I was dressed in my leather jacket and I was walking around the bar and I noticed a gentleman looking at me. I am very introverted when it comes to bars, and so people would have to approach me. And this person I could tell was watching me. After a lot of cruising, he came up in front of me and put a collar on me, and he forced me on to my knees by his side. He didn't say anything and he had the leash on the collar and so I was at his feet on my knees for probably about an hour. He was talking with friends. And at one point, he grabbed the leash and said we're going. I had no freaking clue what that meant. This was all new. He walked me out to his car with his friend, and he opened up his trunk and he shoved me in.

He closed the trunk and got in the front seat with his friend. All sorts of things were running through my head. I was kind of like okay, is this guy really gay? Is this going to be dangerous? I was very lucky. We basically drove to a dance venue, he pulled me out of the trunk, and we went in. It scared the shit out of me because we parked in an alley when he opened the trunk up, and I had no freakin' clue where I was. So we walked into the dance venue. And we went to the bar. He had me on my knees again. I had an agreement with my partner at that time; we had rules when we played outside of our relationship. And one of those was we had a midnight curfew. It was about 11:30 p.m. So I had to tell him that I had to go. He thought a little bit and then he dragged me to the bathroom, into the handicap stall, chained me to the toilet, and flogged me. I was like: *Is this really happening to me? Oh my god! What is happening?*

Then he kicked me.

HE WALKED ME OUT TO HIS CAR WITH HIS FRIEND, AND HE **OPENED UP HIS TRUNK AND HE SHOVED ME IN.**

I SHOW UP WITH INTENT AND I SHOW UP WITH A PURPOSE.

I UNDERSTAND THE POWER BEHIND THAT, AND I ALSO UNDERSTAND THE RESPONSIBILITY OF THAT.

Now, I show up with intent and I show up with a purpose. I impact this community. I impact the trajectory of submissives, slaves, bottoms, dominants, mistresses, masters, like the entire spectrum. I have the ability to touch them with my experiences, and help shape their walk in this space, based on what I shared with them. I understand the power behind that, and I also understand the responsibility of that. There's a responsibility that comes with it. And now I'm showing up with the purpose and the intention to make things better for other people, help them elevate themselves, to learn and grow into who they can be, the better versions of themselves.

PEGSTRESS

PRONOUNS	Xi/She/They/Them	**RELATIONSHIP STATUS OR STRUCTURE**	Single, Polyamorous
GENDER IDENTITY	2S (Two-Spirit)	**AGE**	45
SEXUAL ORIENTATION	Queer	**LOCATION**	Pennsylvania, U.S.

Don't change your lifestyle to accommodate your business. Change your business to accommodate your lifestyle.

x x x

Kink is a lifestyle. It is something that I do for fun. It is a religion. It is a passion. It's my profession. It's my true love. It's all of these things and more for me. Kink allowed me to fully explore my individuality, and really find ways to express it without judgment or without caring what other people think or feel about what I'm doing. Kink allowed that for me.

x x x

I don't have shame with my sex anymore. We've put a lot of shame on sexual acts, on sexual proclivities, on expressions. You know, the common things that people worry about, like: *What are they going to think of me? How are they going to perceive me? How will they feel knowing that this is what I like?* Kink freed me of that and it gave me an arena and other players to have an exchange with where I didn't have to worry about these things. When you're in a space like that, it makes it easier to step out on a ledge, to dare to live your life as you want.

x x x

Kink has always been in me. I always identified it, even as a small child. I knew what it was. I just didn't know what it was. Meaning I knew it was something that intrigued me, excited me, and made me have all of these feelings inside of me, but I didn't know what these feelings inside of me were. I didn't know what kink was tapping into within me.

When I was small, I loved torturing my younger brothers. I took true pleasure in watching my siblings get in trouble and I would usually concoct some type of situation where they would get in trouble and I would be the one to go tell the authority figure so that they could get in trouble and I could get my popcorn, sitting, watching. Knowing what I know about myself now as an adult, though, that right there was the sadism.

x x x

KINK IS A LIFESTYLE. IT IS SOMETHING THAT I DO FOR FUN. IT IS A RELIGION. IT IS A PASSION. IT'S MY PROFESSION. IT'S MY TRUE LOVE. IT'S ALL OF THESE THINGS AND MORE.

CAROLINE | PETER

PRONOUNS	She/Her	He/Him	**RELATIONSHIP STATUS OR STRUCTURE**	Married, Polyamorous
GENDER IDENTITY	Female	Male	**AGE**	34	32
SEXUAL ORIENTATION	Bisexual	███	**LOCATION**	Western/Central New York, U.S.

> I am a masochist, and I am married to a sadist, and we just live it every day.

I am a masochist, and I am married to a sadist, and we just live it every day. It means everything to me. Without it I feel lost. We have so many rules around our relationship; it shapes my life, and it makes me better for it. He controls finances, he controls pretty much everything, and I do all the domestic stuff. And some people see that as bad. But I consented to that when I first started the relationship with him prior to being married. It's fully negotiated out and it is very gendered, and it is very controlling. He controls my entire life, but I let him control my entire life and I enjoy it and he enjoys controlling it.

He controls everything. Everything. Down to like what I wear during the day, what I eat, what I do. As the submissive, it takes all the decisions away. It makes me feel free. It makes me feel kind of uninhibited and unchained to life. I have a lot of anxiety, so him taking those responsibilities over and controlling those things takes anxiety away from me. And emotionally, it's just … it's just so good.

And in sexual play, that is definitely an emotional release for me. Like, if I'm starting to get overwhelmed, we'll sit together and then we'll put it in a play session.

Let me be clear, though. I definitely have all the power. But because he takes his control and he asserts it in a certain way, it still gives me that element I want of having no power. So, there's a consensual non-consent situation. But I do say the word when needed, and it's over, or we pause, and we talk about it. I have the control, for sure.

Our dynamic has changed how I approach people at work and how I am. I'm more assertive. I ask for things that I want more. I speak out about what needs to change. I didn't use to do that. And since he and I have been in this for five or six years, it has changed my approach to work. It has actually improved my work ethic and my productivity.

> Without it I feel lost.

HE CONTROLS EVERYTHING. EVERYTHING. DOWN TO LIKE WHAT I WEAR DURING THE DAY, WHAT I EAT, WHAT I DO. AS THE SUBMISSIVE, IT TAKES ALL THE DECISIONS AWAY. IT MAKES ME FEEL FREE. IT MAKES ME FEEL KIND OF UNINHIBITED AND UNCHAINED TO LIFE.

I HAVEN'T SEEN ANY OTHER PONY PLAYERS IN WHEELCHAIRS, SO I'M GOING TO BE A ZEBRA ON WHEELS AND I'M GLAD I DIDN'T LET MY ILLNESS JUST KEEP TELLING ME I COULDN'T DO IT.

I got sick back in 2017. I was passing out every day because I couldn't keep my blood pressure high enough to stay conscious, let alone stand up. And then I ended up in a power wheelchair. The power chair weighs almost 300 pounds before you put me in it. It's big, its bulky, and has to be charged. It can't get wet. It's got so many restrictions. So I thought: *I'm never gonna be able to do pony play as Mystic Storm again. This part of me is now dead.*

Then last year, in May, we discovered a pedal powered wheelchair, which allowed me to get out of the power chair. And in September, I did pony play for the first time in my wheelchair. And it was amazing. I felt like myself again and I didn't want to stop. I realized that when I had gotten sick with this chronic illness, I became so busy mourning the life that I missed, that I wasn't looking for ways to figure out how to do the things I want.

Once I was able to see that there was a way to do the things I love, I was ecstatic. And I decided Mystic Storm needed a whole new persona. Now, I have a full Rainbow Zebra persona and that's who Mystic Storm is, now in her wheelchair. People ask, "Why a zebra?" And the answer is, because of some of the main diagnoses I have, the medical community calls us zebras, because we're so rare. I haven't seen any other pony players in wheelchairs, so I'm going to be a zebra on wheels and I'm glad I didn't let my illness just keep telling me I couldn't do it.

MYSTIC STORM AKA SPRITE OR CARRIE

PRONOUNS	She/Her/Hers/Ponie	**RELATIONSHIP STATUS OR STRUCTURE**	Polyamorous
GENDER IDENTITY	▮▮▮▮▮	**AGE**	41
SEXUAL ORIENTATION	▮▮▮▮▮	**LOCATION**	Pennsylvania, U.S.

I REALIZED THAT WHEN I HAD GOTTEN SICK WITH THIS CHRONIC ILLNESS, I BECAME SO BUSY **MOURNING THE LIFE THAT I MISSED**, THAT I WASN'T LOOKING FOR WAYS TO FIGURE OUT HOW TO DO THE THINGS I WANT.

WE'RE WILLING TO LOOK AT WHAT THOSE FEELINGS ARE WHEN THAT MOMENT HAPPENS, AND **EXPLORE MORE DEEPLY WHAT THAT MEANS,** SEEKING GREATER ECSTASY IN LIFE.

RIO SPOONER

PRONOUNS	She/Her/Hers	**RELATIONSHIP STATUS OR STRUCTURE**	Legally married to a Woman
GENDER IDENTITY	Female	**AGE**	▮
SEXUAL ORIENTATION	Lesbian	**LOCATION**	Northern California, U.S.

There's a line in a song by Mary Chapin Carpenter that says "there's a keeper for every flame." I think that describes some of the panoply of kink. You can eroticize anything, so you have to embrace everybody. We are large enough and flexible enough to embrace a multitude of people and identities.

Sometimes people will ask me what power dynamics are. I ask them: "Has anyone ever pushed you up against the wall and forcefully kissed you?" That's it. That's erotic power right there. It's just that we acknowledge it verbally and we explore it further; we're willing to look at what those feelings are when that moment happens, and explore more deeply what that means, seeking greater ecstasy in life.

x x x

Kink has really helped give me a stronger sense of who I am. Each step I've taken in my life, whether it's coming out as a lesbian, getting sober, getting into kink, getting into mastery and slavery; each step has taken me closer to who I really am. Because what started as *oh let's go play* has become a very deep part of my development as a woman and as a human being. It's changed my outlook on life and who I am and how I move in the world, and for that I'm profoundly grateful.

I'm a large woman and to the vanilla world I have a fat ass. I certainly got teased about it. I had a guy once use the pickup line of "You have great childbearing hips!" But when I got into kink, my body was celebrated, people wanted to play with me because I had a big ass, saying that I'd be a great spanking partner for them, or that they appreciated I was voluptuous. I wasn't fat — I was voluptuous! I found a lot more body positivity and healing in the kink community than in the general vanilla, heterosexual world.

> I wasn't fat — I was voluptuous! I found a lot more body positivity and healing in the kink community than in the general vanilla, heterosexual world.

HAS ANYONE EVER PUSHED YOU UP AGAINST THE WALL AND FORCEFULLY KISSED YOU? THAT'S IT. **THAT'S EROTIC POWER** RIGHT THERE.

Kink is really about connection for me. It's a space where I get to have a connection with someone. That's kind of the way a kink scene works, right? You get to know someone pretty well, even before the scene starts, where you have that negotiation phase and you start talking, you start learning about each other. What I get out of it is connection both on an emotional level and on a physical level. It's not something I really get outside of kink. It's not something I seek out a lot, mostly due to me being a pretty introverted and anxious person. It also really helps me to get the physical connections that I need, and it really helps me as a touch-starved person.

    It's very powerful for me, connecting to the people who I play with regularly, people who find me attractive somewhat, people who find me appealing to be with, or appealing physically. And that's something that I don't feel a lot in my regular life. The first time it really hit me was when I was playing with someone. And they're saying to me: "Ooh, you're so sexy!" And it genuinely hit me at that time: *Oh my god, people actually view me this way. They actually think I'm attractive.* So that was a huge game changer for me. That's something that gets me going back to kink again and again.

STORM

PRONOUNS	They/He	**RELATIONSHIP STATUS OR STRUCTURE**	▮▮▮▮▮
GENDER IDENTITY	Agender Transmasculine	**AGE**	Mid-20s
SEXUAL ORIENTATION	Queer	**LOCATION**	Canada

IT REALLY HELPS ME AS A **TOUCH-STARVED** PERSON.

I COULDN'T HAVE IMAGINED SUCH A COMEBACK.

MICHAEL HUGHES

PRONOUNS	He/Him	**RELATIONSHIP STATUS OR STRUCTURE**	Married in a 24/7 Daddy/boy dynamic
GENDER IDENTITY	Trans Man	**AGE**	54
SEXUAL ORIENTATION	Bisexual	**LOCATION**	Minnesota, U.S.

> she gave me a safe space to reevaluate what kink was and what it should be, what consent looked like. She turned it all around, all the betrayals that had ruined it for me.

I had a bad BDSM relationship and then an abusive — physically abusive, emotionally abusive — relationship. I was kind of done. I had sworn off the leather community. I thought the BDSM community was just a bunch of abusers, dangerous.

When I met Shay, she was kinky and she was interested in BDSM. And I said there was no way, absolutely not gonna happen, not interested. But we were at about three years I think, and it started happening organically. I would bring her coffee and, you know, do acts of service for her and then we were kind of organically doing it anyway. And one day, she just said, "Hey, you know, let's have a conversation. You know, we're kind of going down this trajectory ... " And so she gave me a safe space to reevaluate what kink was and what it should be, what consent looked like. She turned it all around, all the betrayals that had ruined it for me.

I really would like the story to be told about how one bad experience, about one person ignoring a safe word — and I was injured in the process — could have completely turned me off of kink and anything to do with it forever. I was so adamant that I didn't even want to be friends with people that were into it. I had such a nasty attitude about kink. I caught myself thinking: *It's just a bunch of people with an excuse to abuse people with a blatant intent to hurt people*. But I had an absolute 360 turn because of two people: one bad experience and then one amazing experience. It absolutely made all the difference. Without that trust, I would have missed out on a full life and a whole lot of fun.

Since returning to the kink community, I have run for and won a leather title, and competed at the 2024 International Mr. Leather competition. I couldn't have imagined such a comeback.

I WAS SO ADAMANT THAT I DIDN'T EVEN WANT TO BE FRIENDS WITH PEOPLE THAT WERE INTO IT. **I HAD SUCH A NASTY ATTITUDE ABOUT KINK.**

The more I study kink, the more I explore it, the less I realize I know about it. And if I have to define kink so far, it would be jumping into the hole like in *Alice in Wonderland*. I feel like Alice, literally falling into that hole. And having that multisensory experience where my body, my mind, my desires, my fears, my wants all collide together. My identity as well, is shifting. So I would say that kink for me is a tool, a thing that happened to me and that helped me find my relationship with myself and also with others.

I had a wonderful experience where I managed to tap into a really deep, profound, primal thing inside me. As a Black person who is queer, I've always wondered what it meant to be free. I've always wondered what it meant to have the freedom of perversion. The freedom to actually tap into those things that are seen by society as deviant and not be judged for it harsher than a white counterpart would be. So, when I had the chance to experience that in a safe environment and actually go deep and tap and discover parts of myself that I didn't know, I felt wonderful because I felt for the first time seen, really seen, and not just seen as that Black woman, but seen fully.

> I'm a PhD candidate. I've done so many other things. Being boxed into being a Black queen? I'm like, *Oh, please, be creative.*

So, it was a wonderful experience and I will never forget this, but at the same time the opposite is true: I've been fetishized so many times. For example, with my FetLife profile: On average, weekly, I receive about 10 to 15 messages of people asking me to do race play. I found race play really interesting in a sense that, if the person wants to understand the dynamic that happens during race play, I'm all for it. But most of the time it is someone that would come and be like: *Oh, my Black, Nubian queen —* or *Please, I want to purge my debt as a colonizer.*

It's really annoying, because I think my ego also talks a little bit because I'm like, for Christ's sake, I'm a PhD candidate. I've done so many other things. Being boxed into being a Black queen? I'm like, *Oh, please, be creative.*

LASCARE O

PRONOUNS	She/They	**RELATIONSHIP STATUS OR STRUCTURE**	Polyamorous
GENDER IDENTITY	Woman	**AGE**	38
SEXUAL ORIENTATION	Lesbian	**LOCATION**	France

I HAD A WONDERFUL EXPERIENCE WHERE I MANAGED TO TAP INTO A REALLY **DEEP, PROFOUND, PRIMAL** THING INSIDE ME. AS A BLACK PERSON WHO IS QUEER, I'VE ALWAYS WONDERED WHAT IT MEANT TO BE FREE. **I'VE ALWAYS WONDERED WHAT IT MEANT TO HAVE THE FREEDOM OF PERVERSION.**

dominants flying helicopters out there. It's a funny thing because guys like that are always bottoms. Or, I should say, they're always receivers.

The challenges I've had, the only ones I've had, happened by being in partnered relationships with people who were not kinky, who had so much baggage around this idea of kink, or being a dominant partner, or being a submissive partner. They were so afraid of it. The thing is, we wouldn't have even been together, had I not seen that they have kink within them already. Even having sex with people like that, they like to hold you down, they like to be taken, they like a smack here, a smack there. Yet when we're talking about it openly, they really shut down. That's the biggest problem that I've had: actual romantic partners who can't come out of the kink closet on their own, or don't acknowledge that their own vanilla behavior is actually very kinky. To me it is a real inability to be honest with themselves. That's an intimacy issue.

I'm curious about the future of kink and how that plays itself out. The future of kink is tied to the future in general. How can we be kinder to the earth? How can we climate-change kink, how are we going to get away from leather, how are we going to get away from industrial materials, and what is that going to look like? Or things with sex toys, which are one of my favorite things. How will electronics or technology inform kink? Where will AI take us in sensation play? What will VR bring to kink? These are the things I often think about. How do we reduce harm and increase pleasure?

MARGARET CHO

PRONOUNS	She/Her/Hers	RELATIONSHIP STATUS OR STRUCTURE	▮▮▮▮▮▮
GENDER IDENTITY	Female	AGE	55
SEXUAL ORIENTATION	Queer	LOCATION	Los Angeles, U.S.

I know that I've always been kinky. I know that it's something I didn't even develop, really. It's always just been something I have had an impulse to do. Like ... born this way. There wasn't any real precipitating thing that caused me to sexualize pain or sensation or want restriction or seek a dominant partner or a submissive partner. There was nothing in my upbringing, really. I didn't go to Catholic school ... I don't have a foot fetish. I don't have that kind of thing in general. Fetishism isn't really part of it, either. But I do love the smell of leather just because I've had so many great experiences around that smell.

Kink informs my daily life and makes me very aware of power dynamics overall. In every situation, in every social interaction, there's always a giver and a receiver. I don't like the idea of dominant and submissive because I think that is too loaded. To me, it's more giver and receiver. We sort of look at a dominant as being positive and submissive as being negative. But in truth, they're so equal in my mind. To me, it becomes more giver and receiver, giver of authority, receiver of authority. To me it is more of a sense of how it plays out in my mind and how it plays out in daily life. Both sides are consenting and both sides have 100% responsibility.

What I want non-kinksters to understand is that they probably have some of this in them. And that it is not as "out there" as people think. There are elements of kink that can be really far away from what you do. But honestly, everybody has some kink in them. They're just not calling it that; they're just not facing up to it like that, because I think kink has such a social presence that is really mysterious and ill-defined in a lot of ways. It's not as mysterious as people think, you probably have some of this already. It is one of the most encountered things sexually that you're going to find in any context.

I love that kink is becoming more mainstream. I think, though, it does tend to make it even more misunderstood. Because then you have it as a parody of itself, it just becomes so ridiculous that it doesn't make any sense anymore. When you look at something like *Fifty Shades of Grey*, it's just really funny because there are no male

I KNOW THAT I'VE ALWAYS BEEN KINKY. I KNOW THAT IT'S SOMETHING THAT I DIDN'T EVEN DEVELOP, REALLY. IT'S ALWAYS JUST BEEN SOMETHING THAT I HAVE HAD AN IMPULSE TO DO. SO LIKE ... **BORN THIS WAY.**

I am finding other avenues of reclaiming my culture through Leather as well. This includes using an honorific based in the language I would have heard growing up, and wanting to get a Nehru jacket or something made out of leather for my formals that's culturally meaningful to me. Not that the Tom of Finland look isn't hot, but I know I can take it and make it my own.

SRISANJAY

PRONOUNS	He/Him/His	**RELATIONSHIP STATUS OR STRUCTURE**	Polyamorous, Ethically Non-Monogamous
GENDER IDENTITY	Trans Man / Man of Trans Experience	**AGE**	32
SEXUAL ORIENTATION	Queer/Demisexual	**LOCATION**	California, U.S.

I think what I've found most enjoyable about kink has been exploring energy and authority exchange — specifically the power exchange space as a top. Especially as I consider myself an aspiring Leather Daddy. To me that means being able to provide a nurturing, masculine presence to somebody and help them be the best version of themselves.

I stumbled into kink — generally a couple years before I found my local community. And surprisingly, race play was the category that flipped the switch for me to start exploring it seriously. This happened with a former partner of mine, who was British. As an Indian person, I swear I didn't plan this, but it unlocked something in my brain. We were talking about kink, and I had this feeling come over me out of nowhere and I made a comment about "long overdue vindication" for what their people did to mine.

It was completely spontaneous. I don't know what happened with that. And as their reaction was getting more intense, becoming noticeably flustered, that's when my emotional sadism kicked in: *What's the matter? ... I'm sitting like 10 feet away from you. I don't have my hands on you. Are you feeling okay? What's going on?* We were feeding off each other's reactions ... But we never did that again. That lasted maybe two or three minutes. That was, to this day, the closest to hitting top space the same way people go into subspace. On a scale of one to 10, I'd say that was a six or seven. I'm hoping to get some play that will get me to an eight or nine, so I can see what that full experience will look like.

> race play is one way I can navigate those complex cultural dynamics and history in an empowering way.

Once I got into the kink community, I wondered: *How did I ever live without this? How did I live unaware of this entire other part of the queer community? How is there this part of myself that I didn't know existed?*

I'd be interested in exploring race play further, especially knowing that most likely my dynamics will probably be interracial in some way, shape, or form. As an adoptee to the U.S. from India, I've been estranged from my culture in a lot of ways growing up and not having that connection, engagement, or mirroring. So race play is one way I can navigate those complex cultural dynamics and history in an empowering way.

I AM FINDING OTHER AVENUES OF **RECLAIMING MY CULTURE THROUGH LEATHER** AS WELL. THIS INCLUDES USING AN HONORIFIC BASED IN THE LANGUAGE I WOULD HAVE HEARD GROWING UP, AND WANTING TO GET A NEHRU JACKET OR SOMETHING MADE OUT OF LEATHER FOR MY FORMALS THAT'S **CULTURALLY MEANINGFUL** TO ME. NOT THAT THE TOM OF FINLAND LOOK ISN'T HOT, BUT I KNOW I CAN TAKE IT AND MAKE IT MY OWN.

I've got more kinks than a cheap garden hose and wrestling has been the core of pretty much all of it. Something that I look back on and just laugh at is my situation growing up. I had a reasonably liberal family, especially for Texas, but we were still going to a Southern Baptist Church and all that, so it wasn't exactly a liberal bastion. I would watch wrestling on TV, like WWF's *Monday Night Raw*, or WCW. There is nothing more normal than to walk in on some kid watching pro wrestling, but I was 15 years old, and I knew exactly why I was watching. So to everybody else it looked like totally normal behavior, but I would still watch with my finger hovering on the channel change button.

x x x

As I got more involved in gay life as an adult in San Francisco, I realized something: The distinction between professional wrestling and a drag show is purely academic. You've got men with over-the-top personas, in bright, outlandish outfits, engaging in high drama competition of "who's on top," sometimes with fireworks. It's just that one has more glitter.

CHRISTIAN WALTERS

PRONOUNS	He/Him	RELATIONSHIP STATUS OR STRUCTURE	Married
GENDER IDENTITY	Male	AGE	42
SEXUAL ORIENTATION	Gay	LOCATION	Portland, Oregon, U.S.

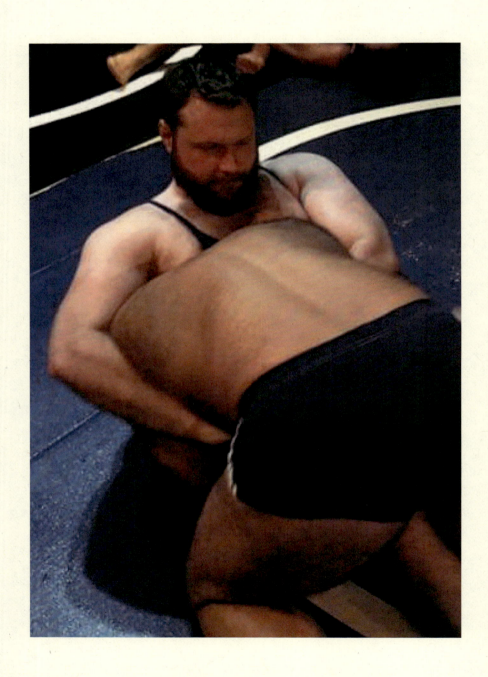

THE DISTINCTION BETWEEN PROFESSIONAL WRESTLING AND A DRAG SHOW IS **PURELY ACADEMIC.** YOU'VE GOT MEN WITH OVER-THE-TOP PERSONAS, IN BRIGHT, OUTLANDISH OUTFITS, ENGAGING IN HIGH DRAMA COMPETITION OF "WHO'S ON TOP," SOMETIMES WITH FIREWORKS. **IT'S JUST THAT ONE HAS MORE GLITTER.**

BEATRICE STONEBANKS

PRONOUNS	She/Her/Sir	**RELATIONSHIP STATUS OR STRUCTURE**	Married, Polyamorous
GENDER IDENTITY	Female	**AGE**	62
SEXUAL ORIENTATION	Pansexual/Queer	**LOCATION**	Bay Area, Northern California, U.S.

Being called Sir is one of my oldest kinks that I didn't know was a kink. My parents had three girls before they had any boys. My dad raised us as boys. He took us fishing and crabbing and we were dirty, playing in the yard while my mother was all clean and girly and frilly and dressed us up. But my father molded my brain and my personality, and it was based on patriarchal, male-dominant nonsense.

My father shaped my early years and men were who I looked up to. I did not have any strong female role models until much, much later in life. All the women were subservient homemakers and uneducated. My mother didn't graduate ninth grade. My father was all about education and reading and words and looking-it-up in the lexicon; he didn't call it a dictionary. I would say, "what does this word mean?" And he would never tell me. He'd say, "look it up" and he'd sit right by my side, and so this level of bringing intellect to the picture was male-focused.

He was a commanding officer on the NY police force, and they called him Sir. It didn't seem like a big stretch to me to want to be called Sir. I identified with my dad, and I loved hearing people call him Sir. As I grew into an adult, the persona stuck. I always played in male-dominated fields. I still do. And I always held men as better than women. I don't anymore, but I did for a long, long time.

x x x

When it came time to be kinky, I was 35. I was vanilla-vanilla-vanilla-vanilla and Christian before that. My first kinky partner, who I fell in love with (you can't help who you fall in love with) was kinky. One day during sex, he said, "Can I just pull your panties down and spank your ass a little?" At the time it wasn't so clear that it felt to me like a man-to-man question, not a man-to-woman question. He wasn't *asking* to dominate my female side, because at that time in my life, men didn't ask women for sex.

I'm ragingly feminine. My main pronouns are feminine. I own my femininity, and I love it. It's just that emotionally and sexually it's Sir. Proudly, it's Sir.

I'M RAGINGLY FEMININE. MY MAIN PRONOUNS ARE FEMININE. I OWN MY FEMININITY, AND I LOVE IT. IT'S JUST THAT EMOTIONALLY AND SEXUALLY IT'S SIR. PROUDLY, IT'S SIR.

I definitely feel like my experience of bondage is very complicated, and that what I get out of bottoming and topping is not the same. Based on my own definitions, rope bottoming is kinkier for me than rope topping, partly because I identify very strongly as a (sexual) masochist. Rope bottoming mostly doesn't excite things that I think of as my own experiences of masochism — pain that is sexual for me. Rope pain is right next to that, but it isn't actually in that box.

Bondage bottoming is usually at least somewhat sexual for me, and bondage topping is less sexual — left on its own. It's not *not* sexual, and it can easily get there. But it certainly isn't more sexual for me than dancing with someone else is. I would personally label the experience of most conventional forms of dancing with someone as being more sexual than rope topping is, for me.

Shibari excites the artistic, fancy parts of my brain, which are very close to the sexual parts, as I expect they are for many people. But they aren't the same part of my brain. I think that's a common experience for a lot of people who are very into Shibari.

JULIE FENNELL

PRONOUNS	She	**RELATIONSHIP STATUS OR STRUCTURE**	Polyamorous
GENDER IDENTITY	Feminine	**AGE**	43
SEXUAL ORIENTATION	Pansexual	**LOCATION**	Washington, D.C., U.S.

SHIBARI EXCITES THE ARTISTIC, FANCY PARTS OF MY BRAIN, WHICH ARE VERY CLOSE TO THE SEXUAL PARTS, AS I EXPECT THEY ARE FOR MANY PEOPLE. BUT THEY AREN'T THE SAME PART OF MY BRAIN.

for trans people. Kink makes me a more open-minded parent, a more open-minded partner, a more accepting human. And so I keep making space for people to be whoever they are, and to be the human that they are. Kink helps me to support them and myself by being more fully human.

JOSEPH KINDRED

PRONOUNS	He/Him	RELATIONSHIP STATUS OR STRUCTURE	Single
GENDER IDENTITY	Transgender Male	AGE	57
SEXUAL ORIENTATION	Gay	LOCATION	The Netherlands

I think being a dom is about taking a certain responsibility for the well-being of anyone that I've been with. I like to go deep, kind of spiritually and emotionally, and I prefer to know people a bit or have a really good chemistry with them to start with. That way, I know what's interesting to them. What is a little scary to them if they want to play on those edges, what's humiliating to them if they want to play with that, and where their boundaries need to be for them to feel actually, truly safe. While we're together, I do feel like my role as a dom is to be somewhat like a lifeguard ensuring the safety of everyone in the situation. So I'm always keeping part of my mind on emotional safety, physical safety, mental safety, spiritual safety. And even if we have a safe word, to always be able to receive a signal for someone to tap out and pause and consider what's going on. I like to pay really good attention, so I can check in with the people that I'm with and make sure that they're feeling good about what's happening or if something starts to come up. I also feel like some of the job of a dom is to be providing aftercare. Aftercare is the idea of how you close out and exit from doing something that might be more intense physically or emotionally or mentally and it really should be what people look at. I think in any sexual or emotional encounters, we need to ask: *How do we kind of gently close that off or contain it? What do people need before they go back out in the world?*

> Aftercare is the idea of how you close out and exit from doing something that might be more intense physically or emotionally or mentally and it really should be what people look at. I think in any sexual or emotional encounters, we need to ask: *How do we kind of gently close that off or contain it? What do people need before they go back out in the world?*

x x x

Kink has brought me deep inside of myself. To know very, very deeply who I am, the quality of my soul, the quality of my thinking. It's enabled me to be more creative and open-minded as I meet people. It's enabled me to really realize that there is incredible diversity among humans … There's a certain way that kink gives me an inner strength to know that if we live vibrant lives, we're going to be more able to survive, feeling persecuted politically, which is kind of the current status

KINK IS

WHILE WE'RE TOGETHER, I DO FEEL LIKE **MY ROLE AS A DOM IS** TO BE SOMEWHAT LIKE A LIFEGUARD **ENSURING THE SAFETY OF EVERYONE** IN THE SITUATION. SO I'M ALWAYS KEEPING PART OF MY MIND ON **EMOTIONAL SAFETY, PHYSICAL SAFETY, MENTAL SAFETY, SPIRITUAL SAFETY.**

I feel like sometimes the stereotype is that kink is dark or weird or sick or wrong. When really, we're just everyday people you meet on the street, but probably more open and receptive. And we probably have a lot of things in common, too … We're just very normal people. It would surprise you the number of medical professionals and lawyers and doctors and students who come to my workshops and they meet each other and they're like: *Oh, you're a grandma too!*

BLUE

PRONOUNS	She/Her	**RELATIONSHIP STATUS OR STRUCTURE**	Single, Ethically Non-Monogamous
GENDER IDENTITY	███████	**AGE**	32
SEXUAL ORIENTATION	Heteroflexible	**LOCATION**	Mexico City, Mexico

After I recently dissolved a relationship, I realized I wasn't getting my needs met to the full potential of my whole sexuality. I decided that when I met someone else, or even just hooked up with someone else, that I wanted that to be a priority.

I ended up meeting someone very briefly, and it turned out, through conversation and negotiation that we both had that desire, so we talked about what kind of practices we wanted. And at that moment, I wasn't experienced in or had any desire for humiliation or degradation play. I hadn't experienced it, or seen it in any form that I felt I was comfortable with or wanted or needed. But this person wanted it, and we talked about it and then we tried it, and it was really eye-opening for me.

> You think that you know what you like, and that you know what you want, but it really opened my perspective on a deeper side of kink, and the heavier side of play, to give myself permission for something new.

I just remember crying so much afterward because I really felt seen and able to enjoy that kind of play. I was really surprised at myself because I had this perspective of my own needs and wants, but was open to exploring my limits with someone. Because that person did it in a really great way, and had the skills to guide me through it in a very safe way, I had this amazing experience.

It became kind of like a switch had turned on slowly, with that specific person. And I really admired it because I received so much pleasure: erotic pleasure, physical pleasure and sensation, and mental stimulation. I'm a very mental person and it really just blew my mind how much I really loved something I had no interest in before. That person and I never had sexual relations. We were just able to exist in this very special space and it really changed a lot of things for me in terms of myself. You think that you know what you like, and that you know what you want, but it really opened my perspective on a deeper side of kink, and the heavier side of play, to give myself permission for something new.

x x x

WE'RE JUST VERY NORMAL PEOPLE. IT WOULD SURPRISE YOU THE NUMBER OF MEDICAL PROFESSIONALS AND **LAWYERS** AND **DOCTORS** AND **STUDENTS** WHO COME TO MY WORKSHOPS AND THEY MEET EACH OTHER AND THEY'RE LIKE: **OH, YOU'RE A GRANDMA TOO!**

Kink has led me into the best experiences in my life. And, honestly, everybody has something. I don't care if it's just the smell of your girlfriend's perfume. You have a kink. Whoever you are, something gets you hot, wet, or hard — something that you didn't expect to. It's exciting and it's fun, and you should embrace it. Because that's really what the kink community is doing. We're embracing the part of ourselves that is not expected. Kink boils down to what works at that moment between two people because it's always about the unexpected connection.

LEE CARL

PRONOUNS	She/Her/Sir	**RELATIONSHIP STATUS OR STRUCTURE**	Married, Polyamorous, Leather Family
GENDER IDENTITY	Female	**AGE**	60
SEXUAL ORIENTATION	Queer	**LOCATION**	Chicago, U.S.

EVERYBODY HAS SOMETHING. I DON'T CARE IF IT'S JUST THE SMELL OF YOUR GIRLFRIEND'S PERFUME. YOU HAVE A KINK. WHOEVER YOU ARE, **SOMETHING GETS YOU HOT, WET, OR HARD** — SOMETHING THAT YOU DIDN'T EXPECT TO. IT'S EXCITING AND IT'S FUN, AND **YOU SHOULD EMBRACE IT.**

For the longest time, I identified as "vanilla" until somebody told me that my sexual practices were actually kinky. And I was like, *Oh, okay, that's kinky?* Seems very banal to me. My definition of kink is probably anything that you perceive to be outside of the mainstream. So that is relative. What I perceive as kinky may seem very tame compared to someone else who is into X, Y, or Z. However, what I'm into may seem very completely out of control and outrageous to, let's say, the average white, cis, heterosexual person.

So I think there's a little bit of a shifting goalpost when it comes to the definition of kink. I think a lot of things that have been described previously as kinky have become mainstream through the advent of the internet, through the normalization of porn.

The kink that I defined for me, is also intertwined with my genders, also intertwined with my sexuality. So it is not a lifestyle. It is just my life. My gender expression is an ever-shifting landscape, and in that landscape are my desires as well. And this is how it interfaces with kink because my desires will manifest themselves very, very differently based on what's happening inside relating to my genders. You know, I could be a very subby masculine person one day and I can be full on demoness from Hades in the next minute. My desires shift along gender lines and they also shift based on who I'm interacting with. So it's like a fluid situation, the landscape is fluid.

DADDYPUSS REX

PRONOUNS	It	**RELATIONSHIP STATUS OR STRUCTURE**	Ethically Non-Monogamous
GENDER IDENTITY	Transgender/ Gender Diverse	**AGE**	42
SEXUAL ORIENTATION	Queer AF	**LOCATION**	Berlin, Germany

IT IS NOT A LIFESTYLE. IT IS JUST MY LIFE.

I think anytime something gives people permission to explore an aspect of themselves, it's a good thing. No, *Fifty Shades of Grey* is not the how-to manual that some people took it as … How it played out and the fact that it didn't demonstrate good negotiation and communication and boundaries and limits, that's not okay. It wasn't an educational book in the first place. It was a fictional fantasy. We forget that. If kink literature actually showed all the negotiation and conversation ahead of time, people would be bored.

> If kink literature actually showed all the negotiation and conversation ahead of time, people would be bored.

ELLEN

PRONOUNS	She/They	**RELATIONSHIP STATUS OR STRUCTURE**	Polyamorous
GENDER IDENTITY	Female	**AGE**	63
SEXUAL ORIENTATION	Queer	**LOCATION**	▮▮▮▮▮▮

> I also think kink is a thought process where we examine distinctly and in-depth our identities, and how we relate interpersonally and sexually with our partners. Most people don't do that.

To me, kink is the thoughts and activities that would not typically be found in very limited sex education and mainstream sex information. That's at least until *Fifty Shades of Grey,* because that changed everything and then everything got weird.

I also think kink is a thought process where we examine distinctly and in-depth our identities, and how we relate interpersonally and sexually with our partners. Most people don't do that. They just kind of glide through life. They find a partner, they get married, they get on the relationship escalator. The difference in the kink community, and the reason that it gives me so much power, is it asks you to do this work and to be thoughtful and to communicate really clearly about where you are and what you want. I struggled with it, certainly. But I asked for it, too. It's a whole other world. It's a whole other ballgame. I think it's beautiful and terrifying to people who don't find themselves drawn to it.

My kink informs and influences the rest of my life 100%. The whole thing about communication and negotiation and thoughtfulness that I live my kink life with has completely infused the rest of my life. It gives me the tools and the skills that I can bring into everything else. Even as a sex educator, when I'm talking to people, I use all types of better communication and negotiation … I happen to think that the kinky world has so much to offer the rest of folks in those skill areas, if people want to hear it and are open to it. I'm not quite sure there's any area of my life at this point that it doesn't touch.

x x x

I can't imagine sex without kink but I can imagine kink without sex.

x x x

I CAN'T IMAGINE SEX WITHOUT KINK BUT I CAN IMAGINE KINK WITHOUT SEX.

> It informs a lot of my life.

my whole identity, but absolutely integral to it. It informs a lot of my life.

We can utilize metaphors in life for learning. Kink has been one of my metaphors. When we talk about things like consent, that's about being a decent human being and caring about someone else. When we talk about exploring our kinks, it's really about being open to new experiences and horizons. When we are trying to learn intricate bondage, it's about passion and focus.

A long time ago — 1980 — I moved to LA and was quite a lone wolf. I got invited to a play party and decided to go. I met a hot guy and tied him up. At some point, after a couple of hours of play and aftercare, I turned around and saw like 30-35 people just gathered and watching, mesmerized. When I play, I am hyper-focused. I don't notice anything going on around me. I am totally dialed in to what I am doing. People asked me how I learned to play that way. I had to be honest: I just learned by watching and by caring. There was never anything official. But some of those people asked if I would teach them, share my approach and skills. The class was ridiculously well-received. This was a tipping point in my life. I became a very, very public kink speaker and teacher, and very quickly. I can't even imagine how many classes I've taught since then. That one party, that one scene, changed my life in such a remarkable way.

RACE BANNON

PRONOUNS	He/Him	RELATIONSHIP STATUS OR STRUCTURE	Partnered, Polyamorous
GENDER IDENTITY	Male	AGE	70
SEXUAL ORIENTATION	Gay	LOCATION	San Francisco, U.S.

My favorite kink usually resides between my ears. And it's usually some form of power dynamics, though that has waned some in recent years. I was very studiously attached to power dynamics, really diametrically opposed power dynamics, with very rigid dominance. Now, I'm pretty utilitarian about my kink, even on my online profiles. I take a more minimalist approach to kink these days. That's to say: I carry a much smaller toy bag than I used to.

I've been actively kinky since I was 17. And I mean that within actual gay male leather culture, not just privately. Privately, it was even before that. But at some point, when I entered kink culture in a way where I wasn't a lone wolf anymore, and I was part of a community, I really got attached to the Dom label, the Dom role. And I liked it. I fostered it. The problem with that is it also becomes a bit of a trap. When everybody in the community knows you that way, and everybody wants you that way erotically and otherwise, it's very difficult to explore outside that box.

I actually use safe signals, more than I use safe words. A common signal that I've used is — and part of it is the mind-fuck of making them do it — to have the sub hold on to a ball, or two balls, during the scene. That's part of the submission, holding on to the ball, like a tennis ball or something. But if they drop it, I know that that's the signal that I need to come in to them and talk.

x x x

> I am one of those kinksters who actually does see kink, for myself, as an identity, pretty much like being gay or any other identity label that I might attach to myself.

By the way, Dave Rhodes, a leather community journalist and editor and publisher of *The Leather Journal,* attributes me with creating the word *kinkster.* I don't know if that's true or not. But he has given me credit publicly as turning the word into the ethos. Maybe so. It's nice of him to say it, at least.

I am one of those kinksters who actually does see kink, for myself, as an identity, pretty much like being gay or any other identity label that I might attach to myself. So even when I am not actively doing it, I'm likely thinking about it. I'm communing with other people who are within the kink community because that's a strong part of my identity. A lot of my community work takes place within the kink communities. It's part of my identity. Not

WHEN WE TALK ABOUT THINGS LIKE CONSENT, THAT'S ABOUT BEING A DECENT HUMAN BEING AND CARING ABOUT SOMEONE ELSE. WHEN WE TALK ABOUT EXPLORING OUR KINKS, IT'S REALLY ABOUT BEING OPEN TO NEW EXPERIENCES AND HORIZONS. WHEN WE ARE TRYING TO LEARN INTRICATE BONDAGE, IT'S ABOUT PASSION AND FOCUS.

> What might be unusual for a heterosexual, monogamous couple could be common practice for a polyamorous, queer group.

For me, "kink" refers to sexual fantasies or behaviors that deviate from what is typically considered normal. This can include overt sexual practices or the sexualization of activities that are usually seen as non-sexual. The concept of "normal" is subjective, varying widely among individuals and communities. What might be unusual for a heterosexual, monogamous couple could be common practice for a polyamorous, queer group.

An anonymous-only, ass-up cumdump might actually consider kissing and spending the night together to be kinky.

Not all of my kinks have to be included in every scene I have, but I do need my play partners to have some basic interest in kink. At a minimum, if I can't spit in your mouth, sniff your dirty jockstrap, or rub my face in your pits, then we're probably not a match for play.

It's important to be on the same page with your play partner(s) and understand each other's limits. Communication, both verbal and non-verbal, is key to identifying boundaries. While it might seem thrilling to show up at a dungeon with "no limits," in practice, this can be dangerous and lead to harmful situations. Pre-discussions about what is permissible regarding pain, leaving marks, and using substances are essential.

While there is no single, correct way to engage in kink, it can often be inspired by what you admire in others and adapt to your own practice. There is no universal set of rules, but consent is the nexus of the kink multiverse.

STEPHAN FERRIS (AKA BLUE BAILEY)

PRONOUNS	He/Him	RELATIONSHIP STATUS OR STRUCTURE	Partnered (open)
GENDER IDENTITY	Male	AGE	37
SEXUAL ORIENTATION	FFaggot	LOCATION	Pittsburgh and San Francisco, U.S.

THERE IS NO UNIVERSAL SET OF RULES, BUT CONSENT IS THE NEXUS OF THE KINK MULTIVERSE.

curious at this point and ask, "How do you feel?" And she came up with one word as her answer. Years later, I had a much older partner. Very similar situation: Tied on the ground on the edge of a staircase. This was actually dangerous, which is what she wanted, right? And I'm pressing down on her with my foot. And I asked her, "How do you feel at this moment?" And she came up with the same word. And that word was *safe*. This boggled my mind. The two women came up with the exact same answer in a very similar situation. But there was nothing about this situation that was safe — tied naked on the edge of the stairs with my boot to their neck. This is the opposite of what almost anyone would call safe and yet that was their experience and it was common between both of them. I still get teary-eyed recalling those situations because of the eeriness of it and because of the beauty of it.

They just knew that *safe* was the word to describe their experience. It runs counter to what many women experience in our culture.

They just knew that *safe* was the word to describe their experience. It runs counter to what many women experience in our culture. Their experience is often one of walking around, wondering whether or not they should be curling up their car keys between their fingers to fend off the next advance that they don't want. Yet these two women find themselves under my boot, naked, tied, and they truly feel safe. And what a contrast, it's mystical. I don't know how else to describe it because it's definitely not linear, makes no sense. A lot of kink makes no sense. It just is.

BONDAGE NEXUS

PRONOUNS	He/Him	**RELATIONSHIP STATUS OR STRUCTURE**	Polyamorous
GENDER IDENTITY	Cis Male	**AGE**	61
SEXUAL ORIENTATION	Heterosexual	**LOCATION**	Columbus, Ohio, U.S.

> These people really do like what they're doing. This doesn't necessarily look like the dangerous thing I thought it might be.

A professor at Ohio State University approached me and said, "Would you come and be a guest lecturer at my human sexuality class at OSU?" That started it, and we went forward virtually every semester for six years in her class. I would drag a Tetris tripod into a classroom of undergrads, with anywhere from 25 to maybe 125 students. And I would take a partner with me, and I would dangle my partner in the air. Then we would both answer questions. And probably the most powerful part of it was when my demo partner, hanging in the air, would field questions from the undergrads. That moment is when the education probably happened and change happened, when their minds were widened into oh … *this is for real!* These people really do like what they're doing.

This doesn't necessarily look like the dangerous thing I thought it might be. If somebody looked at it from the outside, it could look stupidly dangerous, but for us, it was an expression of kink and a very genuine, authentic expression of ourselves. The undergrads would be very quiet for a while as they look at what seems to be — and is — me torturing somebody in the air and with rope. They are very uncomfortable. They are very vulnerable. We are making sexual overtures. And this is a very, very vulnerable space to inhabit right in front of a classroom. The students might project onto my partner as not having any agency, about not really knowing what they want, or of being a victim of me and somehow under my magical spell. They might think it's all about me being dominant and my partner is a person with very low self-esteem. These kinds of projections could come out in the discussion. Then, my partner opens their mouth and talks about how much they pursued this, how careful they are to select their partners, how much time they took to learn about the craft, how long they've been doing it, how they've educated others to do it, and why they're in the room. I can look around and see in the eyes of the students the change that's happening, their minds opening.

x x x

Kink can be so magical. I had two matching experiences I'd like to share. I had a very young partner; I think she was 21 and I had tied her. I got her on the ground and I put my boot to her neck. This is how the scene goes for her. So, I'm really

THESE TWO WOMEN FIND THEMSELVES UNDER MY BOOT, NAKED, TIED, AND THEY **TRULY FEEL SAFE.** AND WHAT A CONTRAST, **IT'S MYSTICAL.** I DON'T KNOW HOW ELSE TO DESCRIBE IT BECAUSE IT'S DEFINITELY NOT LINEAR, MAKES NO SENSE. **A LOT OF KINK MAKES NO SENSE. IT JUST IS.**

I think being disabled gives you a very solid sense of what your body can and can't do, and shouldn't do. I think it definitely affects everything we do. I have Ehlers-Danlos syndrome, that means a laxity in my joints, which means things dislocate a lot. My sub actually has the same disability, which makes things interesting. But we know where we both stand. I also have a coordination disorder, which makes motor control, like spanking, complicated. It definitely changes almost everything. There are certain things that we want to do but know that we shouldn't do, like suspension, for example. It's kink, after all, so you shouldn't have a bad time.

> **IT'S KINK, AFTER ALL, SO YOU SHOULDN'T HAVE A BAD TIME.**

MANTIS

PRONOUNS	He/Him	**RELATIONSHIP STATUS OR STRUCTURE**	24/7 live-in D/s dynamic owner of a collared submissive
GENDER IDENTITY	Trans Masculine	**AGE**	20s
SEXUAL ORIENTATION	Bisexual	**LOCATION**	Prairies, Canada

I THINK BEING DISABLED GIVES YOU A VERY SOLID SENSE OF WHAT YOUR BODY **CAN** AND **CAN'T** DO, AND **SHOULDN'T** DO.

world right now. And so many people seem to be on just a hairpin trigger ready to criticize, judge, dismiss, be enraged. Anything that can help people stop, take a breath, and be aware is a good thing. Kink is one way to achieve that.

> THAT IS PART OF THE REAL APPEAL OF WHAT KINK DOES FOR ME. I FIND IT VERY **THERAPEUTIC, VERY CENTERING.** IT'S BEEN A HUGE PART OF MY **SPIRITUAL** AND **EMOTIONAL DEVELOPMENT** AS A HUMAN BEING.

JASON

PRONOUNS	He/Him	RELATIONSHIP STATUS OR STRUCTURE	Married, Open Polyamorous
GENDER IDENTITY	Non-Binary	AGE	53
SEXUAL ORIENTATION	Gay	LOCATION	Portland, Oregon, U.S.

Kink, for me, is a kind of awareness, through meditation and breath, sitting and being still and focusing on my body. All of those things are very similar to what happens to me when I enter sub-space. When I'm being beaten, when I'm beating someone else. When I'm in tight bondage or confinement, there's a change in consciousness and that is a spiritual, psychic state that I enter. That is part of the real appeal of what kink does for me. I find it very therapeutic, very centering. It's been a huge part of my spiritual and emotional development as a human being. It's just an integral part of my whole experience being alive on the planet.

x x x

> To know that I have the strength to surrender to an intense physical experience, means that I can face a painful medical condition with much more equanimity, without resistance, without fear

I have a neurological condition called episodic cluster headache syndrome. It's often considered to be one of the most painful medical conditions known. The attacks are off the scale as far as what the pain level would be, how you would register that. People who've experienced childbirth and gunshot wounds and amputations and broken bones, say that these cluster attacks are that bad. And I would say from my experience with them, that I really have no choice but to deal with my relationship with intensity, and to come to a spiritual place where pain is an opinion. It is very helpful for me therapeutically. To know that I have the strength to surrender to an intense physical experience, means that I can face a painful medical condition with much more equanimity, without resistance, without fear, without the traumatic stress that often accompanies people who suffer from this disorder.

x x x

I think coming out of a culture that is so patriarchal, and where the power structures we live in are based on control of creative and sexual energy, many people have come to look at sexuality or erotic expression as bad or evil or a sign that they're not good people. If we have the ability to help people explore their own awareness and express themselves in healthy, consensual ways, I think we could do a lot for society these days. There's a lot of anger and outrage in the

KINK, FOR ME, IS A KIND OF AWARENESS, THROUGH MEDITATION AND BREATH, SITTING AND BEING STILL AND FOCUSING ON MY BODY.

There is so much more experience to have in your body and your emotions and the connections that you make with people that you relate to, intimately, erotically, however you think about it. There's so much more there than this limited, crappy "sex education." The sex education most people get isn't education at all. It's just: "Don't do that!"

I tell a joke about sex education: *Does anybody here feel like they got good sex education?* And like one person sticks their hand up, maybe a couple of people. And I say, *Oh, then you must be either a Scandinavian or a Unitarian.* It's so true!

x x x

Vanilla people don't need to do kink. But I do want vanilla people to wonder how do kinksters get to the place where we can do all these things? Well, kinksters understand or try to understand our own bodily experience. And we communicate about it clearly to somebody else and find that they can be trusted with that information, and we can be trusted back. Then we explore. And you can do that and keep it vanilla and have infinitely better sex than you had any idea was possible!

CAROL QUEEN

PRONOUNS	She/They	RELATIONSHIP STATUS OR STRUCTURE	Partnered
GENDER IDENTITY	AFAB & Non-Binary	AGE	66
SEXUAL ORIENTATION	Queer	LOCATION	San Francisco, U.S.

x x x

Another time, I went to a party when I was on my period, and I was wearing a wedding dress that we thrifted, that we cut the whole front out of. Then Robert used the train of the wedding dress to bind me up to a pole and he pulled out my tampon, and left it on the ground in between my feet. He inserted a de-edged knife into my cunt. There wasn't a whole lot of motion, and what motion there was stayed very controlled.

It was a very powerful visual scene, even though it's very simple and quiet. My frigging tampon was right there under me. Any blood that anybody saw was menstrual blood. *But, oh my goodness,* people got very excited. I think for the people around us who were watching it, it must have been kind of a psych out scene, right?

For me it was a trust and an edge play scene because in a scene like that, I mean, I can't imagine doing a scene like that with somebody that I didn't feel like I had the Vulcan mind meld with. It would have to be someone I trusted enough to keep me safe with that kind of danger tool play. I mean, I suppose, doesn't it run through your mental ticker tape: *Any chance this person that I love dearly is a psychopath and I just didn't notice yet?!?* But then once it's over and during aftercare you can say: *Not a psychopath after all. Isn't that nice!*

There are plenty of people who haven't had the opportunity to share or experience themselves in this way at all, and don't have a context where they're likely to get it very soon. The chance to say my body is mine, and when I share it with somebody else, it's a decision I'm making, it's happening because I want to do it. The things that we can do, what we do, are negotiable, are vast and wide-ranging. I might like any of it, some of it, or none of it. I get to determine that for myself.

x x x

Kink is roaring, erotic energy.

x x x

> **Kink is roaring, erotic energy.**

I had not been given space as an assigned-female-at-birth, female-bodied, and largely female-identified person out in the world, to embrace a sexuality, an eroticism, that fully held limits. So, a piece of kink play, for me, involved the largely universal permission and even expectation and responsibility to define and explore and express my limits. So, in a space that vanilla sex had never actually articulated for me, kink did articulate that. And part of why kink has been so extremely important in my life was not just giving me somebody's individual permission and support around expressing those kinds of sentiments but a *cultural* support. This was a revolution for me personally.

One of the things that was extremely important to me in my pre-kink/proto-kink, and kink incarnations, as an erotic person, was exploring, just figuring out what I liked. I heard other people describing intense sensation play in extraordinary and transformative terms, and, ultimately, I determined that I either hadn't found the proper context for it, or it just wasn't the way that I was wired. At least compared to the excitement that I got from the D/s piece of play.

How would I have known one way or another, right? I needed space for exploration to know my own kinks. All kink or vanilla erotic sensation-seeking, anything excitement-seeking, anything happens in its own context, right. And everybody's context is a little different.

x x x

> **This was uproariously hysterical and so hot, all at one time.**

I went to this party by myself. And I think it was my first BDSM party. Someone I knew complimented my newly blonde hair, and I enjoyed that. And I was in my cute, pointy little high-heeled shoes and my little sexy outfit, and David put me in bondage, standing bondage, with my hands over my head. Pretty simple. And then he took one of my shoes off and spanked me with it. It was such great fun. It was so hot. It was so funny. It was all kinds of mixed things. This was uproariously hysterical and so hot, all at one time.

THE SEX EDUCATION MOST PEOPLE GET ISN'T EDUCATION AT ALL. IT'S JUST, "DON'T DO THAT!"

Nate:

I'm kind of obsessed with kink, it's fair to say. I like to spend almost all of my free time reading about it, talking to people about it — to friends, partners, strangers, to folks on social media. It's a huge part of my life these days.

    I was closeted for many, many years, and deeply ashamed. And it took me many years to overcome that. I did a lot of obsessing about kink back when I was closeted. And it was like, Oh my gosh, there's something wrong with me. And that was kind of constantly weighing me down. Now it's like, Yeah, I love it! So I am going to do it all the time and talk about it and explore it. It's now been three years of that and not showing any signs of waning. And then, of course, my intimate relationships are defined by and centered around kink.

K:

At times, today's kink culture annoys me, it makes me anxious, it gives me some serious heartburn. I'm tired of people cosplaying something that is part of my deepest freaking identity. And then they do it poorly, and they talk absolute bullshit, while trying to gatekeep stuff they don't know anything about. It's about being authentic. I mean, this is not a Halloween costume. And I am absolutely offended by the fact that people treat it that way. I just want to smack them. They think that BDSM is all about big dudes beating the hell out of their wives. And that fem-doms are all about failed men who are wormy and crawling around on the goddamn sidewalk and aren't even human anymore. If you're a dominant in any gender, you're running around in leather gear, and insulting everyone who comes in your path. I hate all of it. It pisses me off, to no end. Lord, please let's make things a bit more comfortable so you don't lose your job if somebody outs you, or you don't lose your kids because of somebody else. Let's make it a bit more legitimized.

NATE & K

PRONOUNS	He/Him | She/Her	RELATIONSHIP STATUS OR STRUCTURE	Polyamorous, married to nesting partner
GENDER IDENTITY	Man | Woman	AGE	48 | 52
SEXUAL ORIENTATION	Heterosexual | Bisexual	LOCATION	Pacific Northwest, U.S.

I'M TIRED OF PEOPLE COSPLAYING SOMETHING THAT IS PART OF MY **DEEPEST FREAKING IDENTITY.**

> There are two worlds of kink. There's the POC world of kink, and then there's what the rest of the world sees: white kink.

There are two worlds of kink. There's the POC world of kink, and then there's what the rest of the world sees: white kink. I've attended quite a few events where I was the only person of color at the event, and it is awkward, very awkward.

My husband is Black also, so we made a conscious effort to start searching for Black events because fetishization of Black people is rampant in the white kink world. And that's always been a struggle with me. I've always been of the mindset that I don't like to separate things. I want them to come together. I want to go to an event where there's a healthy mix of Black people and white people, and not just one or the other. It's not necessarily that Black kink doesn't exist. It's that it exists in a separate world. We are on our own. We go to our own events. We have our own people who we connect with, and then there's white people and they have their own. I want to bring everyone together.

The fetishization of people of color in kink situations is very common. Once you know what to look for, you see it a lot. It's disturbing. I've had a lot of people come up to me, because they assume I want to be fetishized, and then they get upset when I'm like, Hmmm, no. It's the same as if you assume someone's into CBT, and you just walk up and ask if you can kick them in the balls. You just don't do that. It's a heated topic that no one wants to talk about it, and the only ones who want to talk about it are the people who don't see anything wrong with it.

CHILUNA

PRONOUNS	She/Her	**RELATIONSHIP STATUS OR STRUCTURE**	Married, Polyamorous
GENDER IDENTITY	Female	**AGE**	40
SEXUAL ORIENTATION	Heteroflexible	**LOCATION**	Ohio, U.S.

I grew up in a religious household where certain things were not acceptable or were seen as shameful. And when I came into the kink world, it was almost like no matter how depraved I thought I was, there was always someone else that would be more. And it's not necessarily that I don't feel shame, but I don't carry that burden so much. Because I know that it's what I enjoy. It brings pleasure to me, so why should I be ashamed of what I'm doing with myself? I'm not forcing myself on anybody else. I'm not forcing my desires on anybody else. So why should I feel shameful for making me happy?

I do burlesque dancing now. This was not something I would have done 20 years ago. I'm more outspoken. I demand things for myself more.

I think of myself as demisexual or closer to asexual, which I always thought might make me weird. Like in school, I couldn't figure out why everything was so sexual for everybody.

x x x

> So being hetero-flexible is like this: There's cake and then there's icing. For me, men are the cake, and the women are the icing.

I have an analogy for my hetero-flexibility. So being hetero-flexible is like this: There's cake and then there's icing. For me, men are the cake, and the women are the icing. Some people enjoy cake and icing. Some people can sit in the corner and go ham on the icing. I enjoy cake with a little bit of icing on it, every once in a while. Sometimes I just like cake. I like women physically, but I'm aromantic with women. I am dominant with women. I'm more submissive with men. Which is also why, for the way my brain works, when I am submissive, I'm more sexually aroused. When I'm dominant, I'm less sexually aroused, and it's more about the mental game. I do enjoy playing with women, but it's difficult for me to explain to them that I don't play sexually. So I will do things to them. They can't do things to me, because I don't get turned on by it. It's all about the dominating and the control. It's not about the sex.

x x x

WHY SHOULD I FEEL SHAMEFUL FOR MAKING ME HAPPY?

TURNING THIS PAGE IS AN ACT OF CONSENT.

partners. Some of the photographs have been adjusted to highlight a point or create interest for the reader. Sometimes, we were asked to mask an identity because we still live in a world of bigotry and discrimination.

We took great care to include desired names, gender identities, sexual orientations, and other personal identifiers. If you notice text blacked out or left blank, that represents the caution many kinky people must still exercise depending on their comfort level, life situation, or location. Not everyone can be entirely out about their kink, and we didn't want to leave a false impression that everyone can be.

People learn from their and others' past experiences. We want our readers to learn so their future experiences with kink, to whatever extent they embrace it, are better, safer, more fulfilling, and more fun. There is physically and emotionally healthy kink, and there is unhealthy kink, too, just like with everything else in life. Encouraging more of the healthy variety is our aim.

The closing section of the book is titled "Aftercare." While not every person interviewed specifically mentioned aftercare, the kink community guideline of aftercare directs that we all take care of ourselves and our partners after play — as well as before and during it, too. Aftercare's importance was sprinkled throughout the interviews. We thought it was a lovely way to close out the book. We have been with you throughout and want you to know who we are. It's our way of being present with you.

If you're new to kink, welcome. If you're an experienced kinkster, welcome. If you randomly picked up this book, welcome. Perhaps perusing this book will nudge you to embark on your own journey. Regardless of where on the kink spectrum you do or don't reside, we hope learning about the fascinating experiences of our interview subjects will give you an appreciation and education of kink and about real people, living real lives, in real ways. At the very least, we hope this may serve as a metaphor to inform and improve your own life.

Please enjoy, read, and learn that *Kink Is* ...

heritages, ethnicities, and origins helped us inform and craft our perspectives, but our whiteness and individual identities require us to state all this up front. Working on this book has been transformative for the entire team. We have benefitted from the gift of those who trusted us and shared their stories.

We cannot possibly know in advance if a topic we cover here will elicit an uncomfortable emotional response from a reader. When discussing a topic frankly and honestly, one person's experiences or language might be considered triggering to another. Any strong reaction, we hope, will encourage questions, learning, and understanding. Sometimes rough emotional terrain can help us emerge better on the other end of it, and that is our hope: That you might question, learn, and understand in new ways, just as we did.

Even within kink communities there can be instances of sexist points of view about women or nonbinary people, regarding their roles, presentations, appropriate sexualities, and so on. If such perspectives are given here, it's simply to give the reader a realistic view of a set of communities that are imperfect as are their members. We have not sanitized away the challenges we must confront.

The vernacular and conventions used within kink communities and the world at large change and evolve. We've made every effort to employ the most responsible and accurate terminology available to us. At times, someone we interviewed used a specific term, and we honored them by maintaining it in their text as articulated. Even emotionally charged words have often been left within the text because those are the words many people encounter in real life.

As you read some of these stories, you may notice some questionable decisions or opinions expressed. Trust your gut instincts when you encounter such material. Some of our interviewees were quite honest that they were often lucky that a situation hadn't gone badly. We felt it important to present even questionable experiences as cautionary tales. Look upon such stories not as educational per kink community standards but rather educational as in the "do not try this at home" sense.

As you read, you'll probably think to yourself that a certain aspect or realm of kink isn't discussed. That's not by design but simply the result of the interviews organically going where they went. We did not approach this project with an agenda to cover every possible expression of kink. Rather, we aimed for authenticity of experience, however it was shared.

The photographs included here were provided by the people interviewed. They reflect a choice made as to how to best present themselves or their kink

What did we ask our interview subjects? We allowed the conversation to evolve as the discussion unfolded, but we prompted each person with some standard questions which included:

- How do you define kink?
- Does your kink inform and influence the rest of your daily life?
- Is there one kink experience that stands out as notably wonderful, life changing, or as a cautionary tale for others?
- What do you most want non-kinksters to know about kinksters and kink communities?

Depending on the answers, and the natural, organic interjections of information and experiences, we let the conversations flow as naturally as possible. We wanted people to share their own voices and stories, not just answer our prompts.

Many told us of their origin stories, those first instances when they knew they were kinky. Or they told us about their first kinky encounters and how those proved formative for their subsequent explorations. No two stories were the same. No two people were the same. That becomes clear as you read the words of our remarkably generous interviewees.

After we began the editing process, the book developed and morphed. It became what it is through our continued interactions with the people we interviewed. Their honesty, transparency, and generosity in sharing of their lives and experiences honed the content and format as much as our team did.

The entries presented here are largely random. That's by design. Each story is unique. Enforcing a rigid order could have implied that one person's story was more important than another, which is not true.

We acknowledge that this book, and the associated documentary film project now in development, has been shaped by a production group of cisgender white people. We recognize that as a limitation and a place of privilege. For deeply complex and unfair reasons, we have been granted the cultural permission to ask such questions and seek such answers, where others would not have been allowed to do so. We have worked to be sensitive and inclusive, though we assuredly have our own blind spots and oversights. Numerous people from other

Some engage in an array of activities, while others define their play by a single act or mindset.

Some people in the book are monogamous. Some are non-monogamous. Some are polyamorous. Some are partnered. Some are not. Many of the people interviewed are in relationships with a partner who isn't kinky. This reflects the realities of the world and how relationships aren't always in perfect synchronization. The breadth of relationship styles and configurations run the gamut, because kinksters run the gamut.

Some here identify as heterosexual, pansexual, gay, lesbian, bisexual, trans, or intersex. Gender identities and expressions run the gamut from specific to fluid.

Various faiths and cultures are represented, too, clearly illustrating that kink is a pervasive desire and practice among people across the planet, even if how that kink manifests might vary culture to culture.

People of all ages and body types have been interviewed because we know the youthful, curated images presented by social media, advertising, and entertainment are not accurate mirrors of the everyday human. Some interviewed have physical or emotional challenges they work with, and they have found safety and accommodation in certain styles of sexuality and community.

While sex is integral for many of those interviewed when engaging in kink, others distinctly separate their sex and kink needs. That may be a surprise to some readers. Kinky practices are often, but not always, sexual. Others fluidly alter their incorporation of sex with kink and vice versa. Yet again, the variety of perspectives was vast. You'll notice the range of kink activities, rituals, priorities, and mindsets people enjoy vary dramatically. Kink is not any one thing. Kink is ...

Tastes vary. So do kinks. So do kinksters. Just like the rest of humankind.

We also came to realize that over time the landscape in which kink exists has changed. Society has generally become more accepting of kink activities and those who participate in them. Media portrayals have become more common and positive, though plenty of kink shaming and kink fear still gets presented. We aim to add to the positive through real-life human experiences and to replace the fear with curiosity.

Despite some problematic aspects, the success of *Fifty Shades of Grey* sparked explorations into sexual variations on a broad level. Still, the books and films based on it presented kink, BDSM, and power exchange relationship dynamics in some ways not endorsed by the educated and active kink communities. The reality is far more nuanced, careful, and responsible.

of kinksters around the world. Hundreds upon hundreds of people filled it out. From those entries, we selected what we considered a representative subset to complete our one-on-one interviews. Not everyone we approached or asked was interested in talking with us. We respected their decision and only moved forward with folks who consented to going deeper with us.

Each person interviewed was recorded in a secure manner and the interviews were fully transcribed for our team to review. We then identified specific passages or quotes that seemed to best represent that person or the aspect of the kink experience in which they navigate. We had each participant review and approve their content featured in *Kink Is*. A few folks decided not to move forward with their story at that point, too. We respect their decisions, without reservation. That is how consent works.

Please note that whether the book contains just a single quote from someone interviewed or a few paragraphs of narrative, we don't consider one interview to be better than another. Each participant had an abundance of history, experience, and insight to contribute. Sometimes the gist of an entire interview could be encapsulated in a single quote. At other times it needed more context. All of those interviewed were generous with their time and transparency. We thank them, each and all.

Our team made every effort to reach as diverse a cross section of kinky people as possible. Kink is universal as is much of its culture and norms. That's one of the repeating themes we noticed during the interviews. By interviewing people from Australia, Canada, Columbia, France, Germany, Italy, India, Mexico, and the United States, among other locations, we hoped to identify commonalities as well as differences, and we did.

As we conducted these interviews, the first surprising realization was that despite our team's experience with the topic — ranging from a relative newcomer to those with many decades in the community — we discovered erotic interests, and their associated cultures, that transcended the stereotypical or expected. Those we interviewed answered our questions and told us stories which reinforced that we're all unique humans walking the planet. Each succeeding discussion proved that point. Yet, commonalities consistently appeared.

While some of the people profiled here navigate within robust kink communities, others indulge their sexual tastes and desires in private. While some describe themselves as full-time kinksters, others simply punctuate their regular day-to-day lives with occasional forays toward alternative sexual horizons.

Kink Is, our title, was inspired by the wide variation of answers to our questions: *Kink is what...?* At the same time, kink actually just ... is. It exists. It thrives. It grows. It influences. It connects. It's a natural phenomenon, and we celebrate it here.

One of the first questions we asked each person was: "How do you define kink?" Not a single person offered the same definition. Not one. Each person saw kink differently. Each person experienced kink differently. Each person manifested their physical and mental kinks differently. Like the fingerprints, snowflakes, plants, and landscapes of nature, no two are alike. We had to conclude that no two kinksters are alike. We even asked: *Does kink actually exist? Or is all of this just the unique expression of human sexual experience most don't discuss?*

A guiding principle our team kept in mind throughout the entire project was the idea of "emotional voyeurism." Sure, kink is often about certain fetish garb or physical acts, but the essence of why it delights is the emotional impact it elicits, both internally among participants and externally among those who witness it directly or indirectly.

Reality was the watchword of this book, not the sanitation of people or communities. If you read something that makes you balk at its safety, level of consent, or sound decision-making, it's offered here for how it is, not how it should be. Without confronting the truth, we can't improve and grow. We have attempted to be both responsible and fearless, like most of the kinksters we know.

If you meander through any kink community for long enough, you'll repeatedly hear the word "consent." That's because it's a cornerstone of what kinksters do in interacting with each other. If there's a single foundational concept we hope to instill in readers, it's consent. Well, that, and fun. It must be fun, too.

Consensual kink is not assault. Kink is not violence. When someone says no, it means no. Nonconsensual coercion or manipulation is never okay. Informed and negotiated activities are the gold standard of healthy kink sexualities and communities. And, we would suggest, of good relationships and life in general.

There is not one right way to be kinky or one focus of kink that's better. So long as everyone participating expresses initial and ongoing consent and enjoyment, then you are doing kink correctly. That includes respecting when consent is withdrawn during play, as is sometimes the case.

Kink communities have evolved to include and respect consent and this project honored that foundational principle. At the beginning of this process, we circulated a survey as widely as possible to solicit feedback from a vast array

INTRODUCTION
How this book came to be

Welcome to the diverse and richly complex world of kink. *Kink Is* highlights some of the people and practices making up the wonderful communities many of us rely upon for acceptance, support, and security.

This book contains a series of first-person narratives — excerpts taken from hundreds of recorded interviews with people from all walks of the kink community. The participants were vulnerable, honest, and proud during our discussions. Any initial assumptions about the directions this project would take were overcome by what we heard and learned. The world of kink was revealed as much larger, more nuanced, and increasingly varied than we ever dreamed. Those who shared their stories provided us a tremendous gift of insights. We are honored to share their gifts with you.

Consent is fundamental to kink and what is described in this book. Be assured, each participant featured gave their informed consent to be included in these pages.

Kink Is presents adult content. Everything offered here is simply intended to show how kink manifests in real people's lives. This book is inherently most appropriately read by people able to make conscious and informed decisions about the material they want to read.

This book celebrates the "not normal" and the "un-usual" of the erotic realm. That's not a slight or a degradation of any kind. In fact, we suggest that it's the deviations from what's perceived as typical where the greatest beauty is found. Perhaps that's true of sexuality as much as it's true of everything else in life. Like it or not, practice it or shun it, kink still exists even if many might say it's not normal. So be it. Simply put: *Kink Is*.

Our hope is that as you read, you'll *feel* something: Maybe moved or seen, perhaps curious or engaged. Emotions underpin what makes life worth living. By experiencing the range of emotions offered – or provoked – here, we hope your life and sexuality will be enriched. An overarching emotion that emerged throughout the development of this project is one we hope you'll experience too — *joy*. No matter the form it may take, the ultimate objective of kink play seems to be joy. That may be an assumption for some readers; it may be a revelation for others.

FOREWORD

I think kink is normal. It is way more normal than normal. Normal is abnormal, as far as I have experienced. Normal is perverse, and the kinkiest kink of all. Vanilla is a flavor and white is a color, but they're not my favorites. I'll take a Salted Caramel Vanilla if I need to and maybe an Antique Linen will work for a closet wall that needs repainting. But for sex — plain, unadorned, passionless pumping purely for procreation — I would rather not do it.

"I want to get off like everyone else gets off" is, for me, such a weird point of view, truly because nobody really gets off in the same way. No matter what is said, what is sworn to, what is shown in movies — nothing and nobody is really that normal. Nobody does it the same way. And anyone who says they do is lying. Maybe lying because they are afraid of asking for what they really want. Or maybe just because they don't know what they want. They never took the time to find out. Perhaps nobody bothered to ask. If no one has asked you — then take the time to ask yourself! What do you want? I mean - really, really want? It is something we should know. You don't have to share it, unless you want to, but at least tell yourself your secret.

What makes us unique and what makes sex interesting is that everything for everyone is their own. We each have our own body with its own history and its own way to express love and passion — a song of yourself only you can sing and then maybe harmonize with another at times. And sometimes, when we harmonize with another, it becomes an even more beautiful piece of music because in the union, we become whole — or a hole — or whatever.

I love sex because I love the vast experiences my body can enjoy. I love kink because I know the way to pleasure is not always in a straight line. I love the people in this book because they have found their way to the special place they inhabit and can take others there with their stories. The way we are kinky is far more normal than the ways we are normal.

Margaret Cho

Publisher and Editors Disclaimer

Kink Is depicts and describes graphic sexual content throughout. It should be read only by persons of legal age and in geographies or localities where permitted by law. Readers are responsible for ensuring that accessing and reading this content is legal in their jurisdiction.

This book is intended to be educational and informative but not instructional.

In exploring and documenting the world of kink, the publisher and editors gathered first-person narratives, which reflect the individual choices, practices, and actions of the people who shared them. Some of the depicted and described scenes and events in this anthology should be considered dangerous and potentially harmful to persons unfamiliar with how to engage in such activities.

Safe, sane, and consensual kink practices require focused education and careful skills development. Engagement in such practices should not occur without full awareness of associated risks nor without fully informed consent. As readers learn about the world of kink, they are cautioned not to engage in anything depicted or described in this book until and unless they know how to do so while maintaining their personal safety. Persons with mental health concerns should seek professional guidance before participating in any depicted or described activities as part of ensuring their own safety. Readers are encouraged to consult with experienced professionals in the kink community for proper guidance as they make their own personal choices.

Unbound Edition LLC and Divine Deviance LLC disclaim any and all liability that may arise from reading about the individual choices, practices, and actions shared herein by the persons describing or depicting them, and specifically from any and all actions that readers may engage in as a result of reading these stories.

KINK IS

Johnny	328
Tatiana	332
Graylin Thornton	336
Aspero	338
Susan Wright	342
Liztli	346
Spencer Bergstedt	350
Penny	356
Nora	360
Jay	364
Maura	368
Pepper	370
Francine	372
AFTERCARE	376
Race Bannon	378
Patrick Davis	380
Jörg Fockele	384
Lola De Milo	386
Adam Ouderkirk	390
Beatrice Stonebanks	394
Acknowledgements	398
Photography Credits	402

Lola	220
Karen Ma'am	224
Tyger Yoshi | Tyger's slave	228
Mikey	234
Coco	238
Papa	242
Ruby Ryder	244
Lyle Swallow	248
Fennec Fortune	250
Ayzad	254
Janet W. Hardy	258
Mr. Allan	264
Inanna Justice	266
Flicker	272
Buffy Lee	276
HiThereCatSuit	278
Nunca	282
Sir Ivan	288
JimJam	292
Sir Guy	296
Diablo	300
Slush Puppy	302
Rain	306
Zero	308
Miss Pearl	312
Queen Cougar	314
Tua	320
Gudrun	324

Sakura	122
Captain Kink	126
Gaz	128
Stacey Diane	132
Master Kayne | Bambi	134
Dolly	138
Alexander Cheves	142
Fred	148
Caritia	150
Rio	156
Paul Rosenberg	160
Master Devyn Stone	162
Ian	166
Sky Russell	168
Lady V	172
Sven	176
Alistair LeatherHiraeth	178
Rebecca Orchant | Sean Gardner	182
Koki Vieto	186
Jessamy Barker	192
Marilyn Hollinger	196
Ivo Dominguez, Jr.	200
Slave Slime	202
Catasta Charisma	204
Felicity Azura	208
Moss	212
Peter Tupper	214
Riptide	216